Transcend

Angie's Extreme Stress Menders

Volume 4

©2016 Angie Grace. All rights reserved.

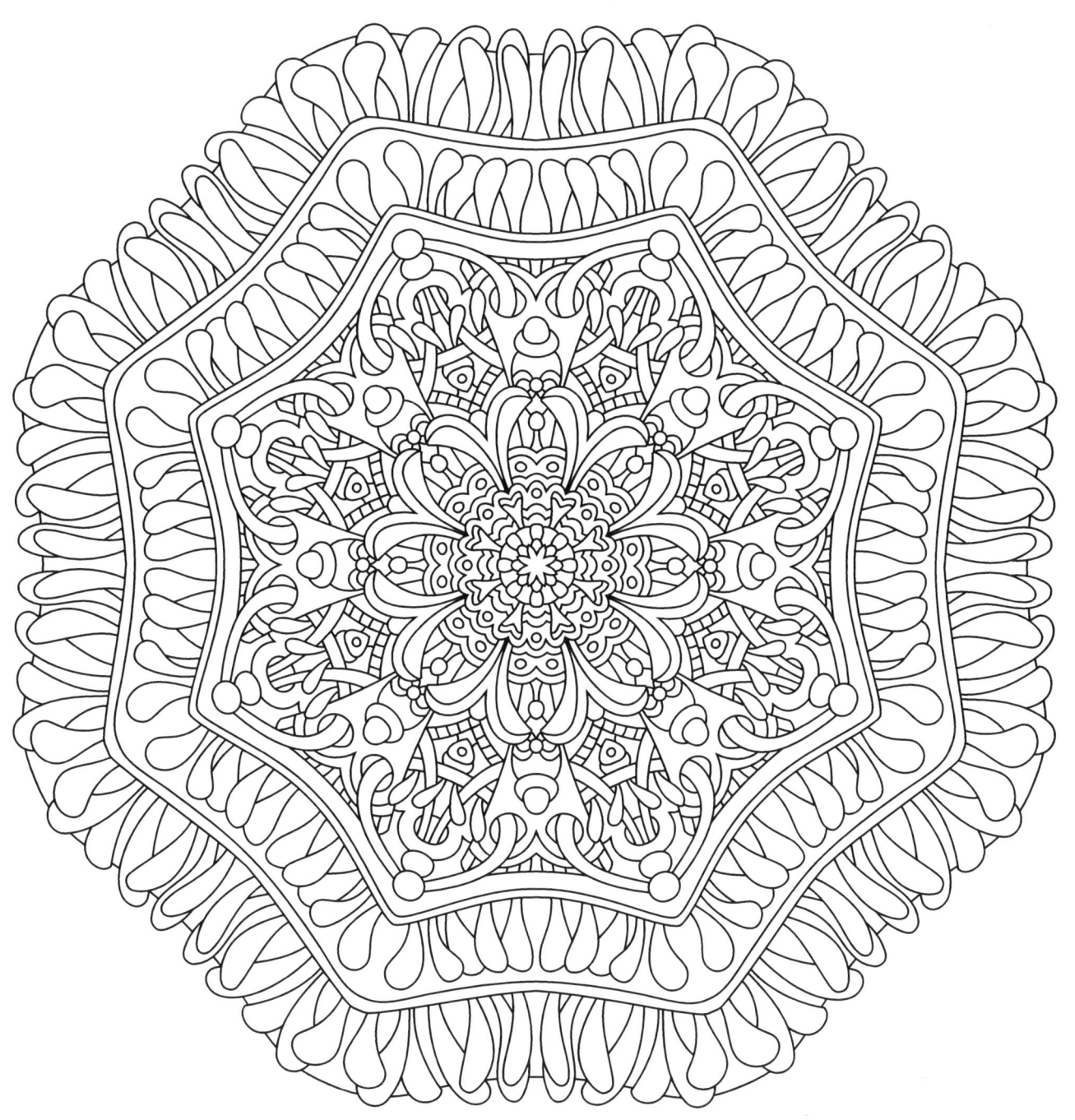

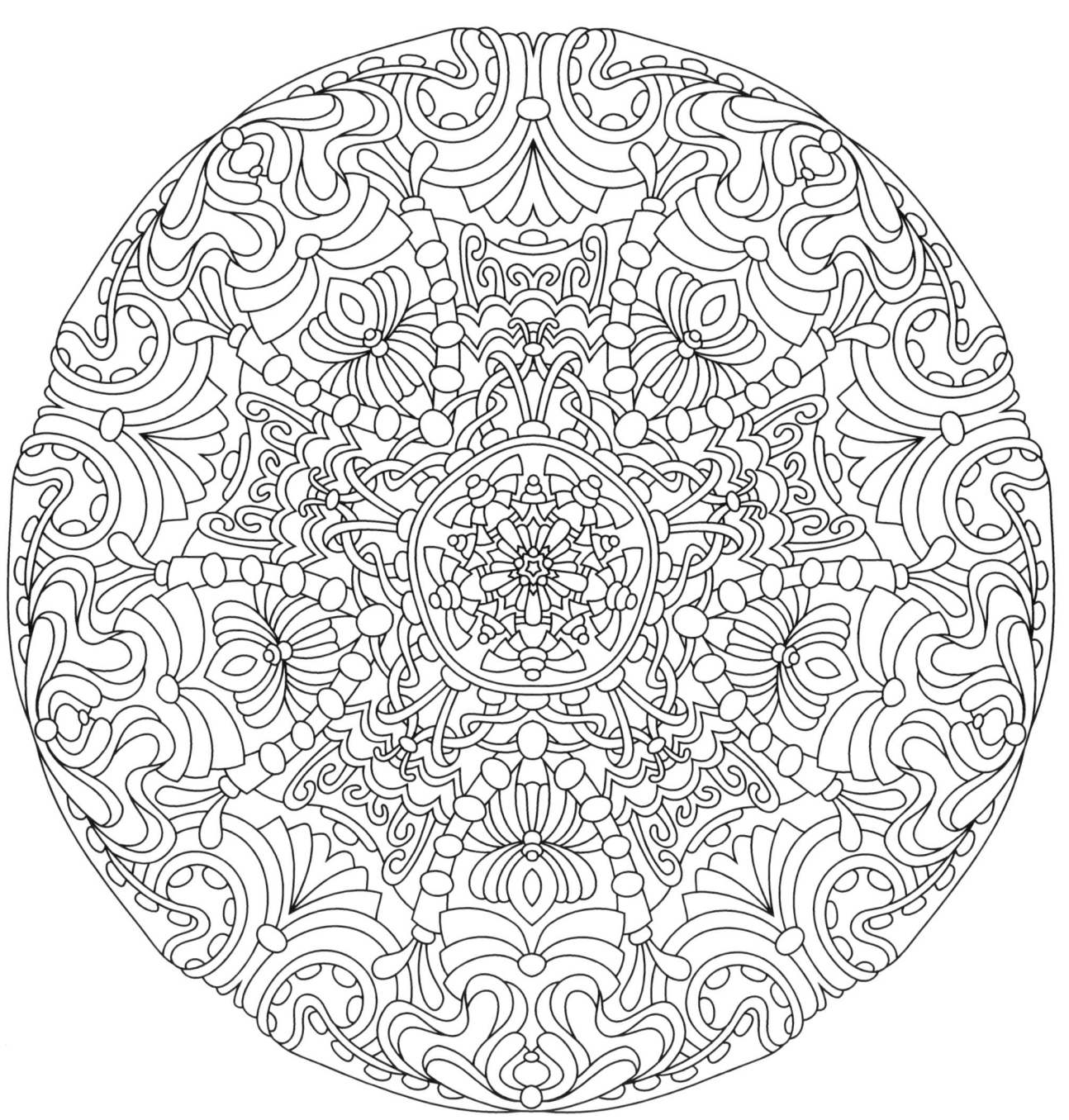

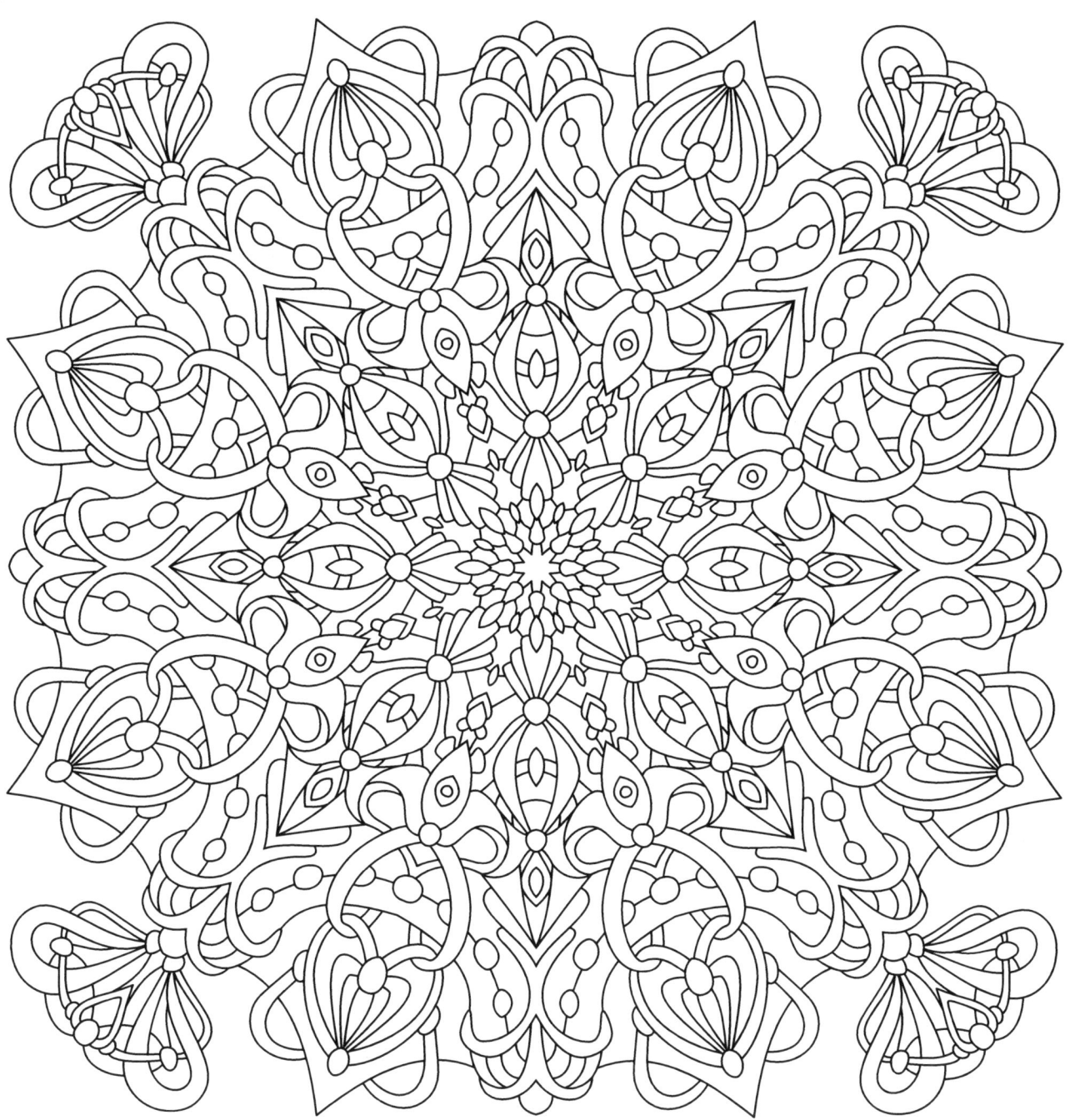

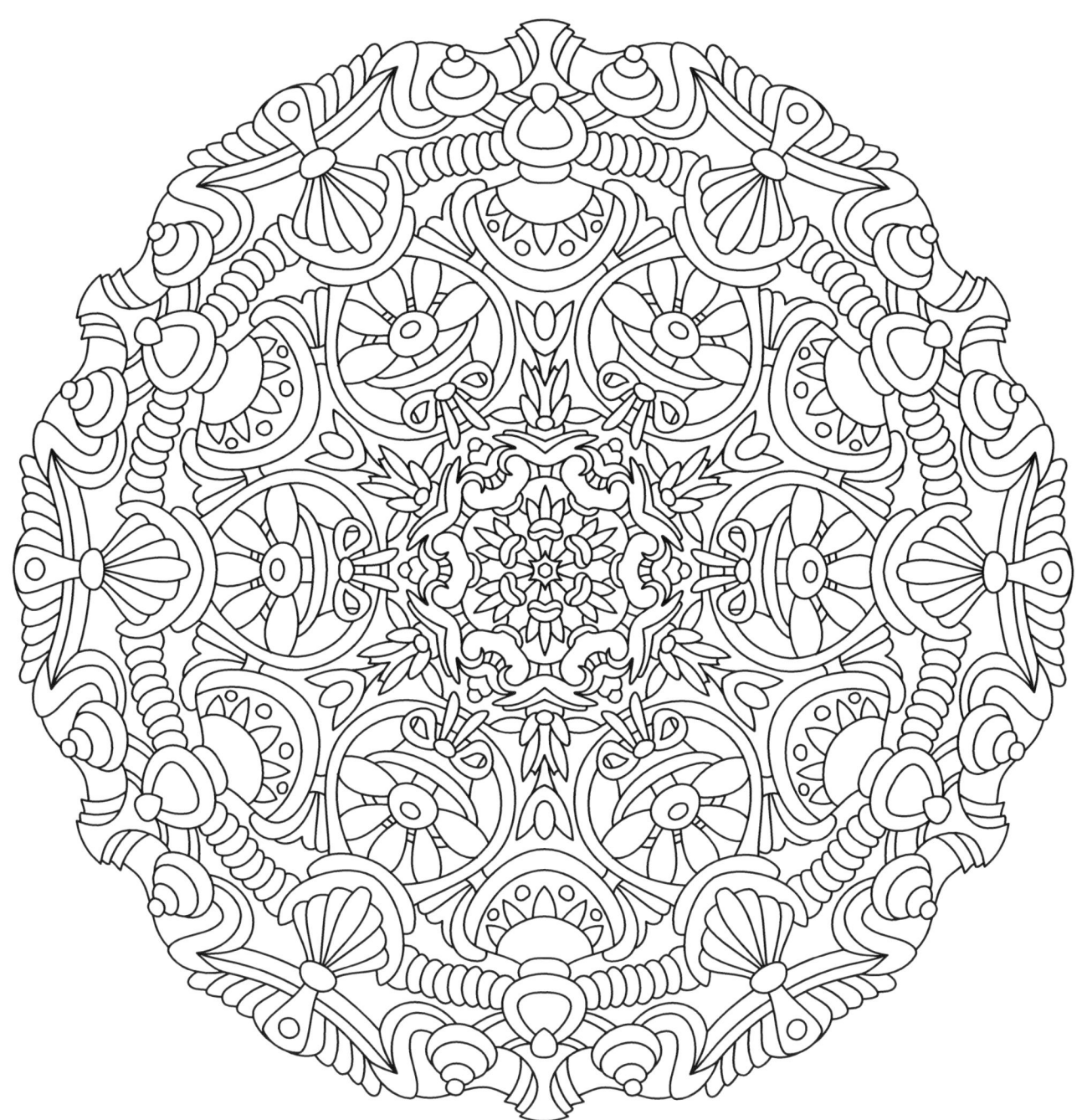

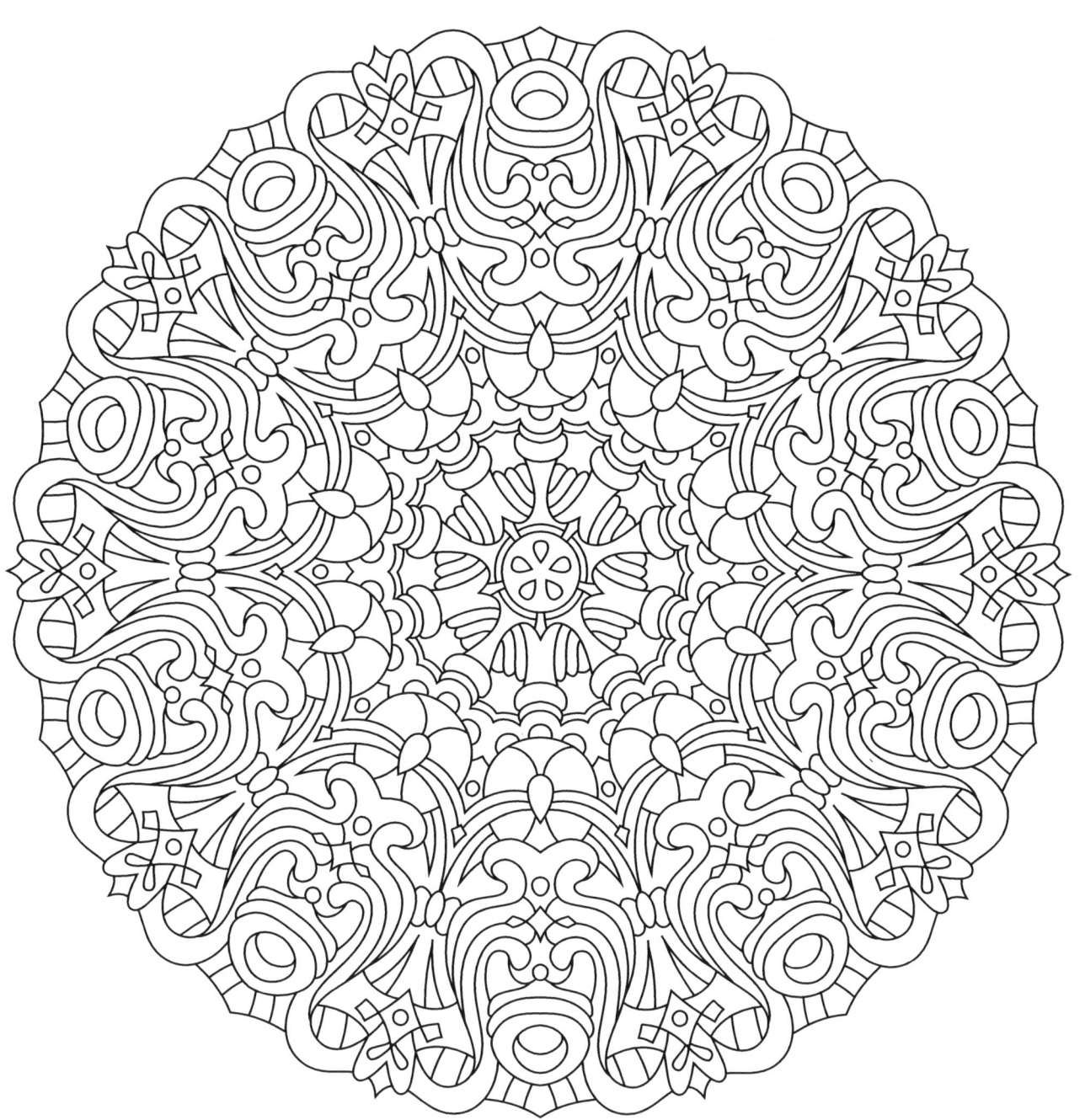

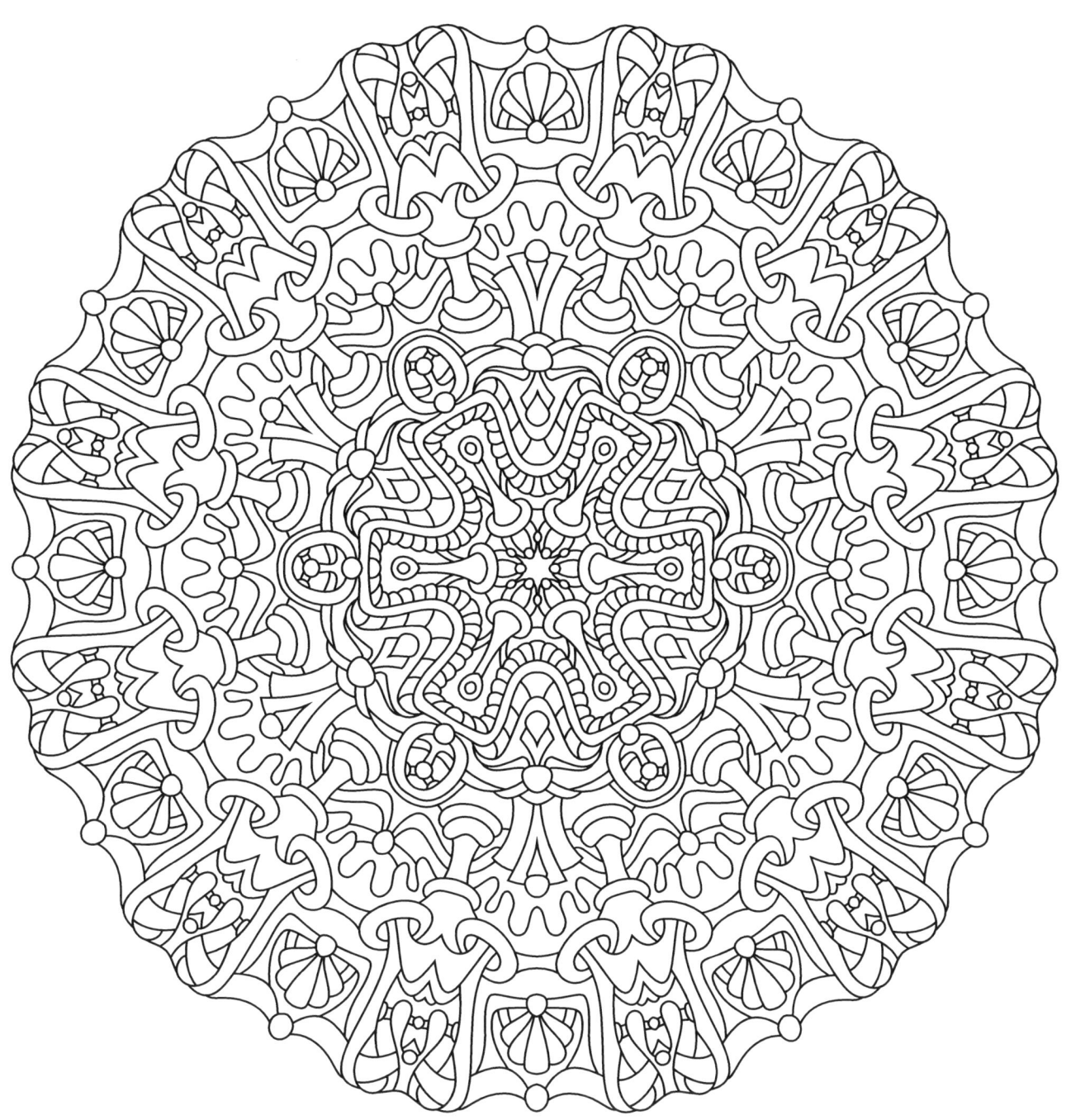

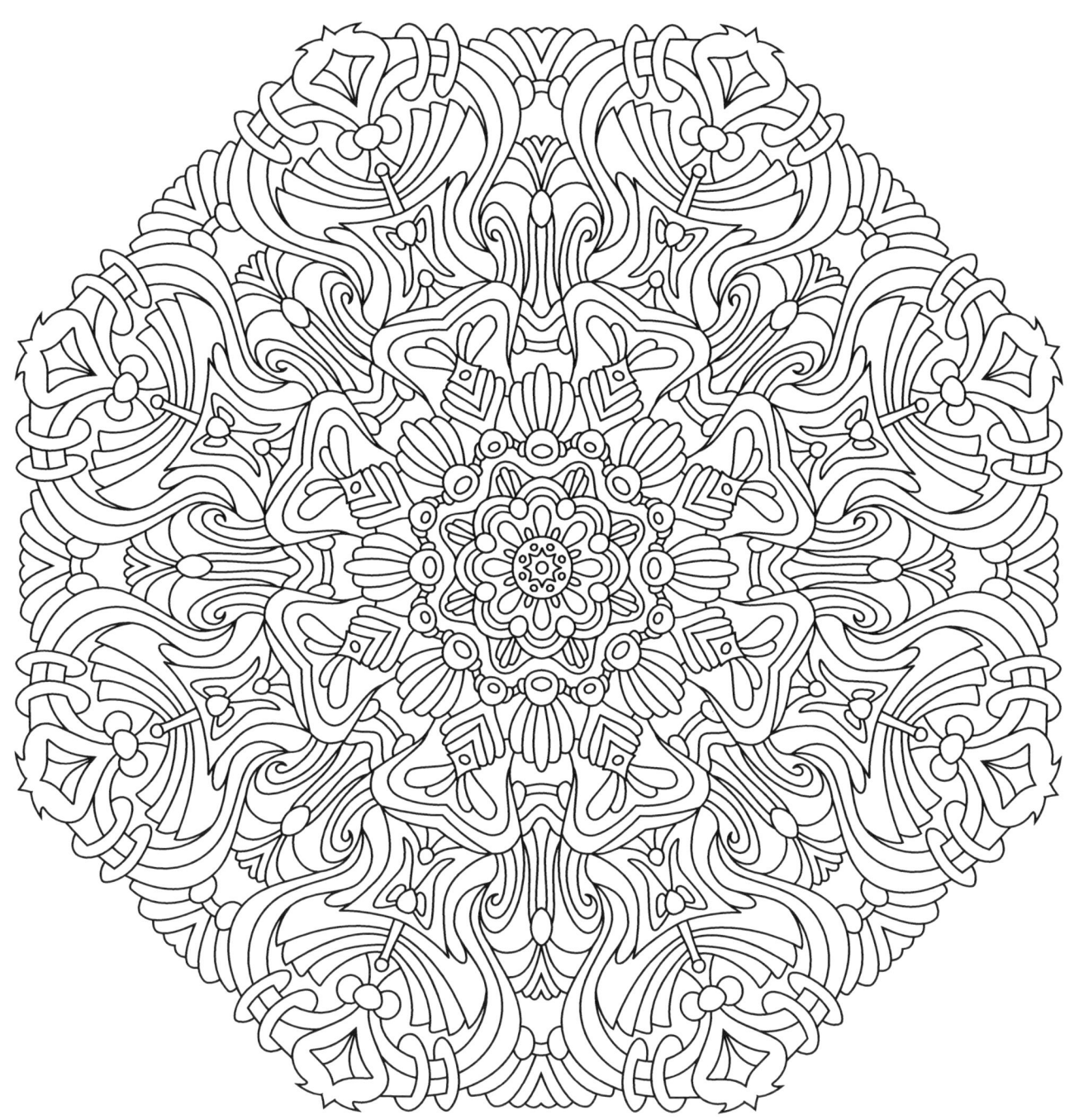

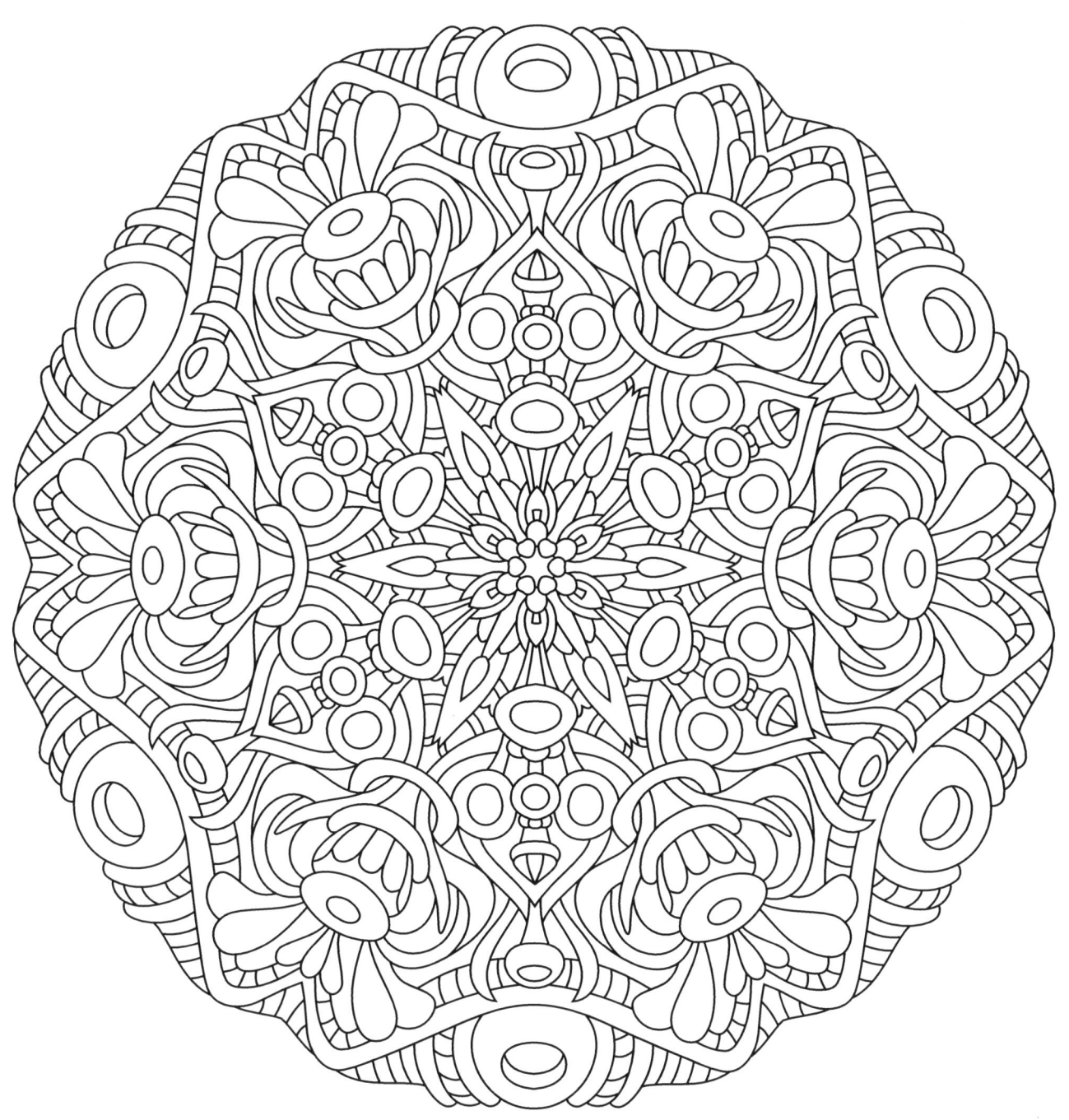

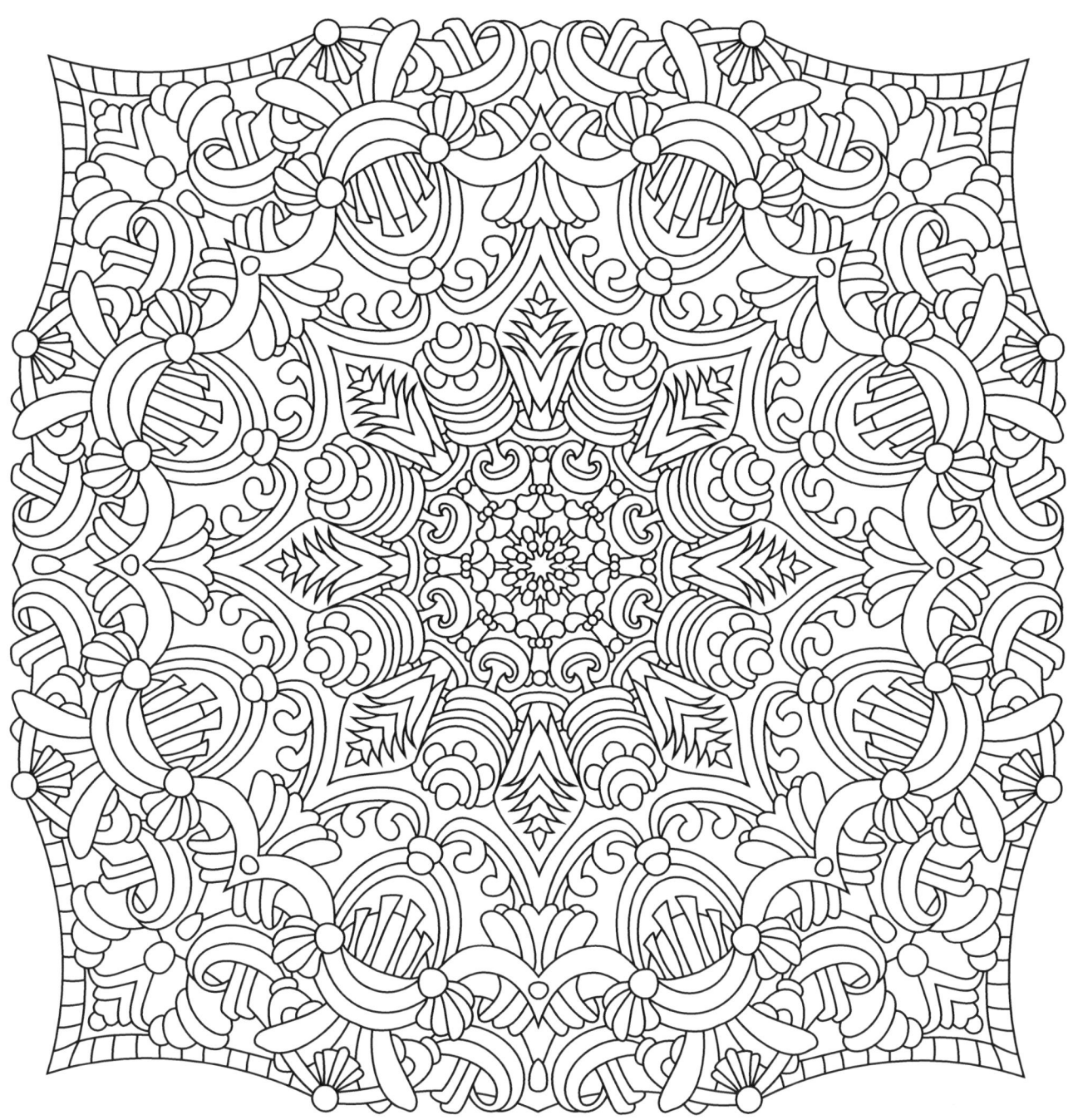

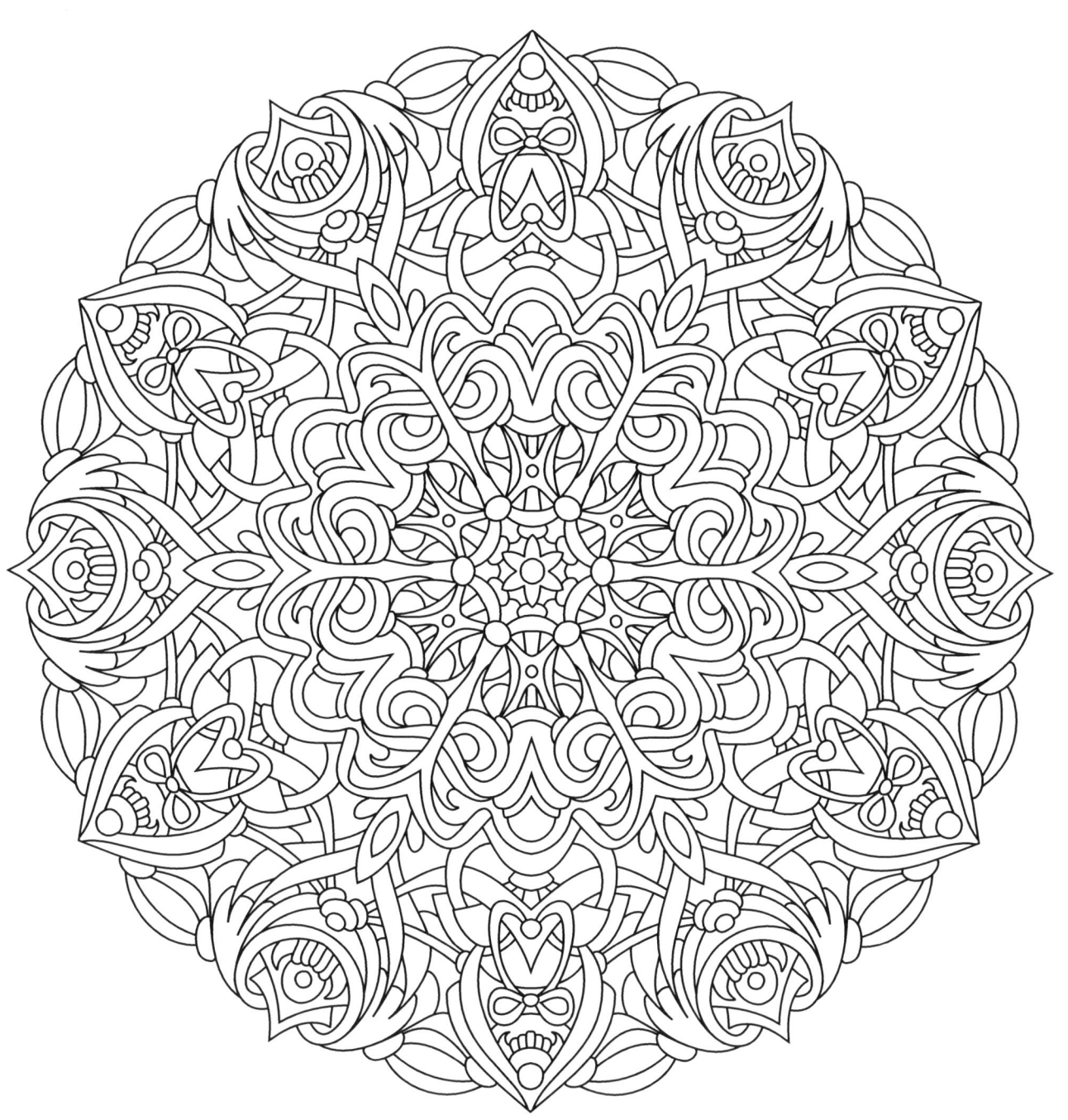

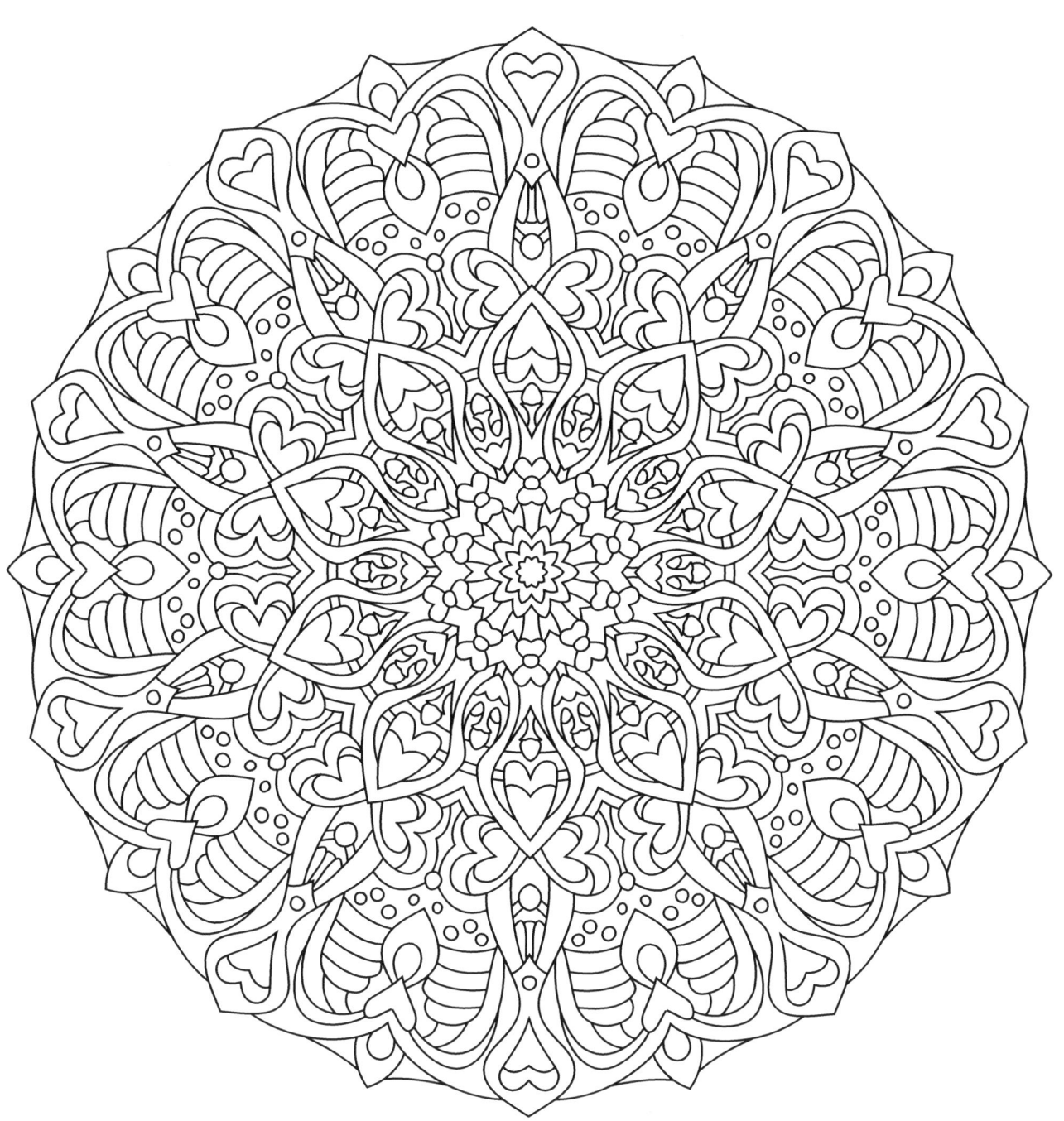

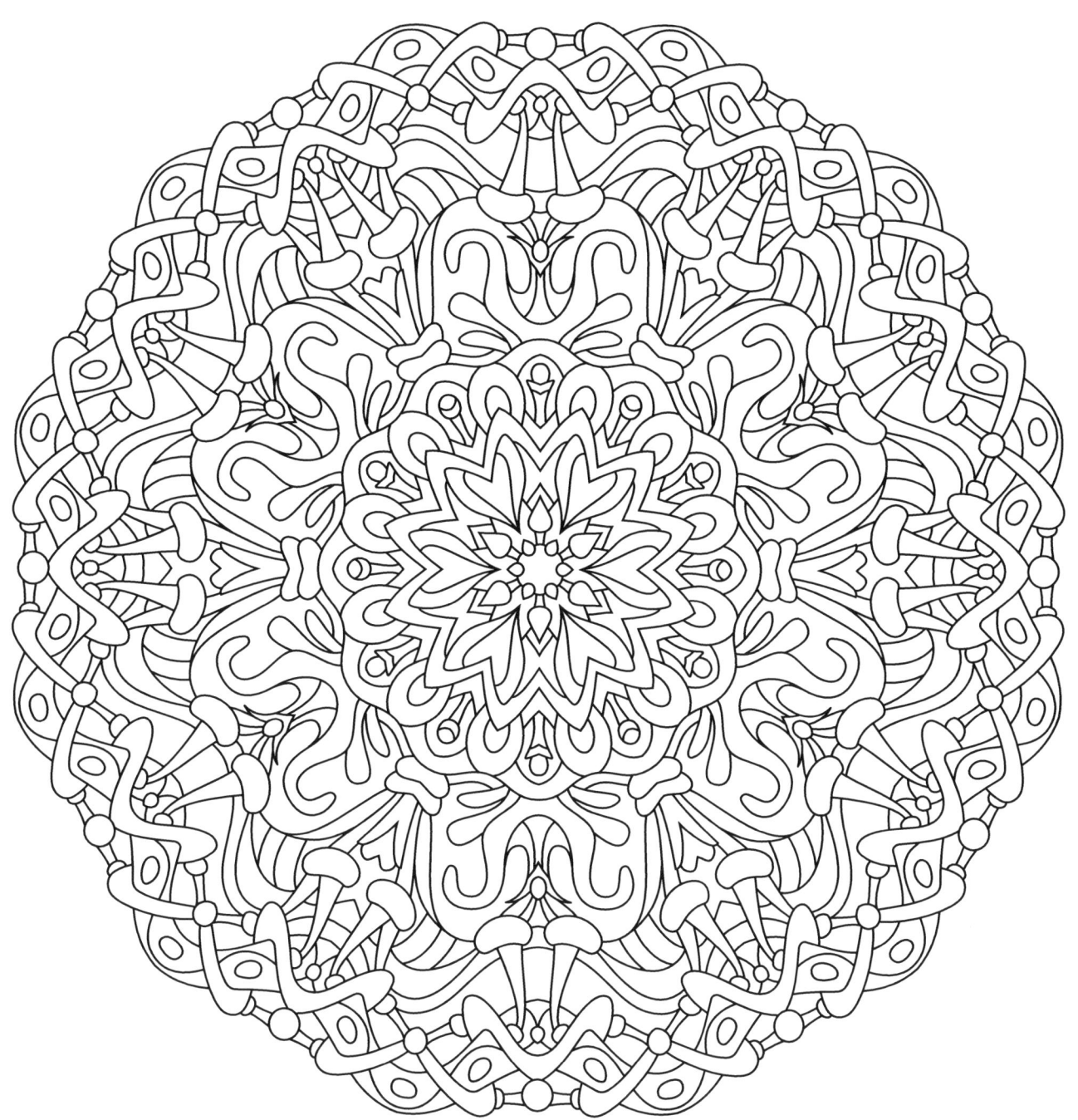

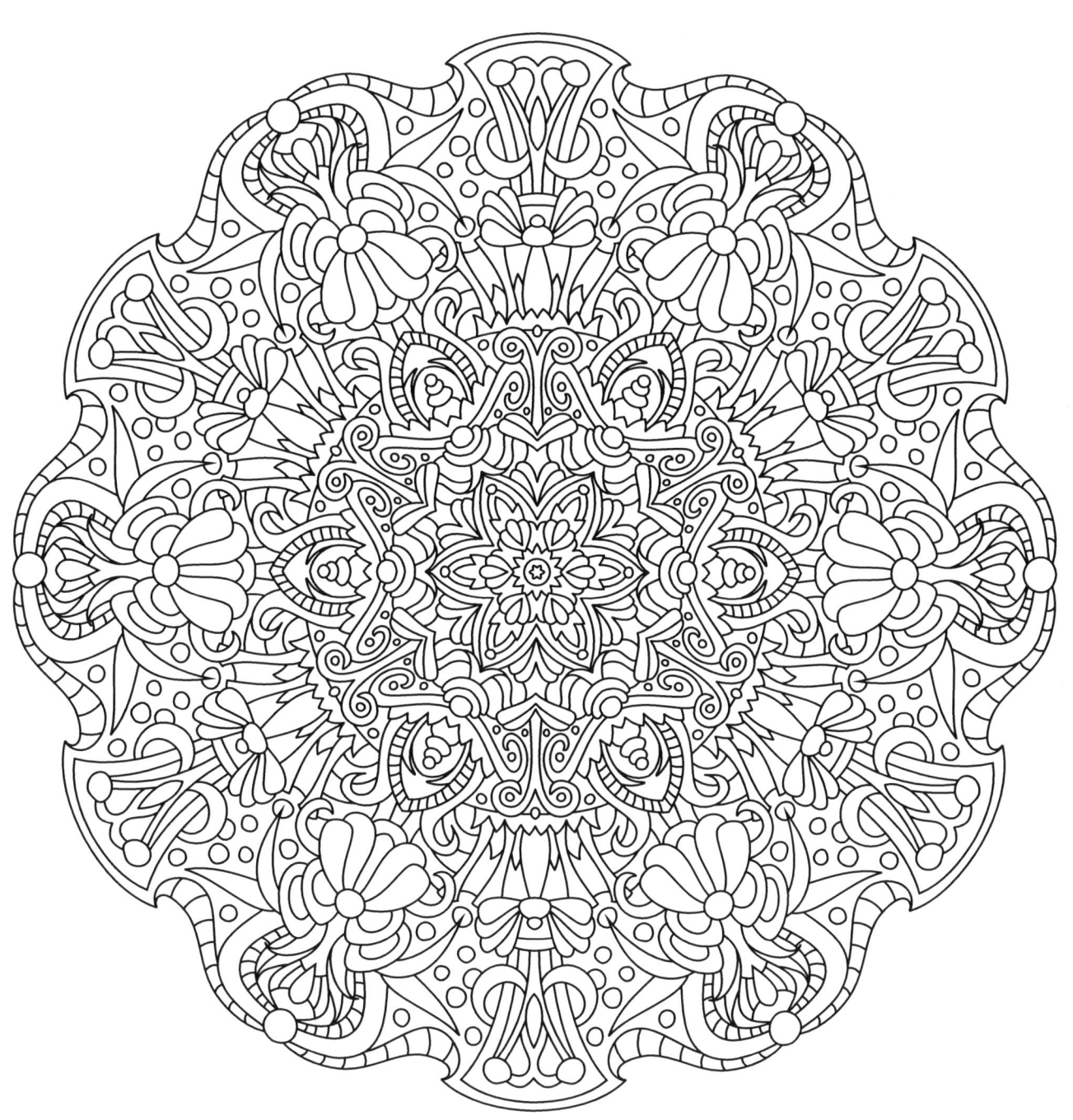

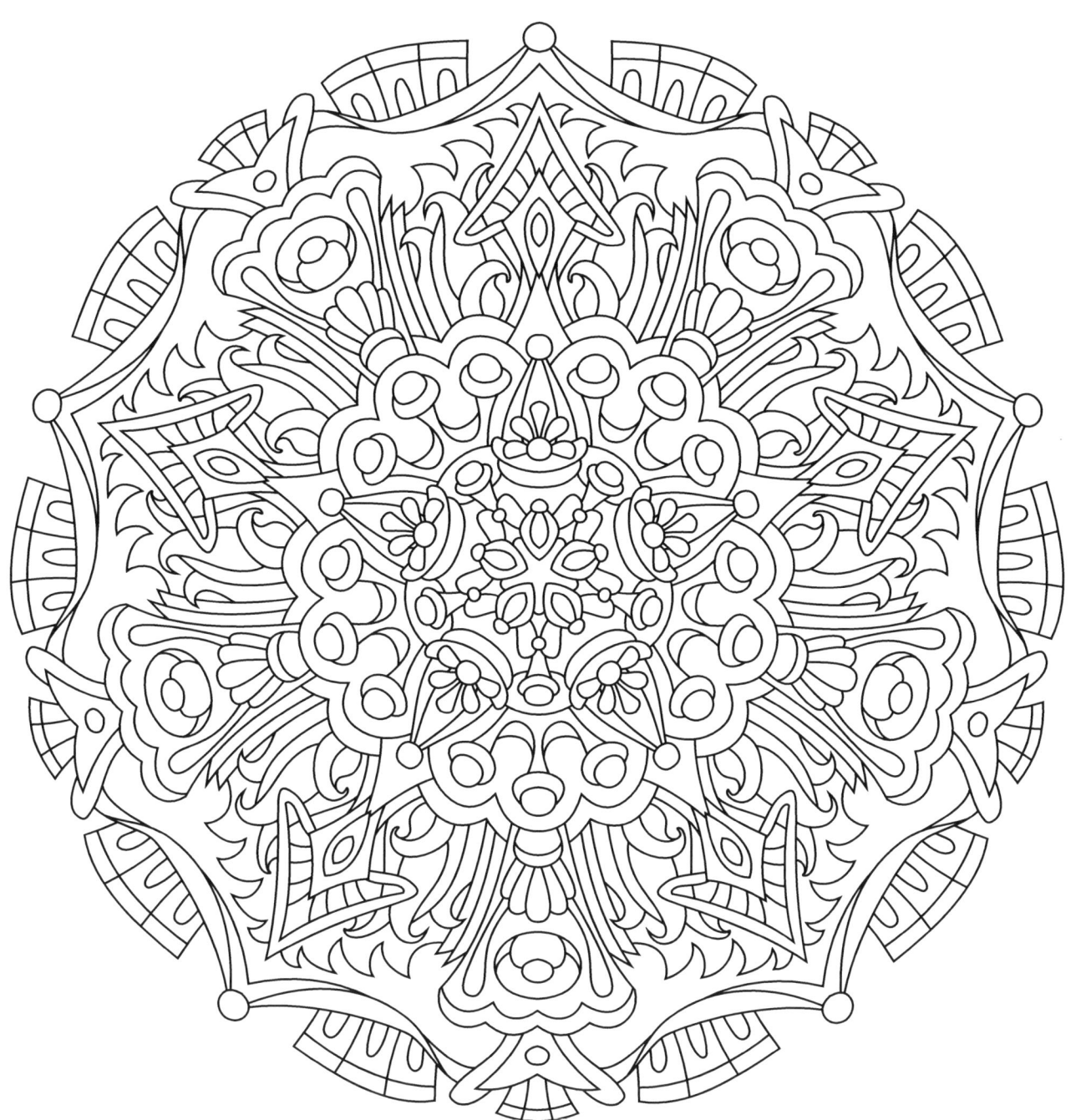

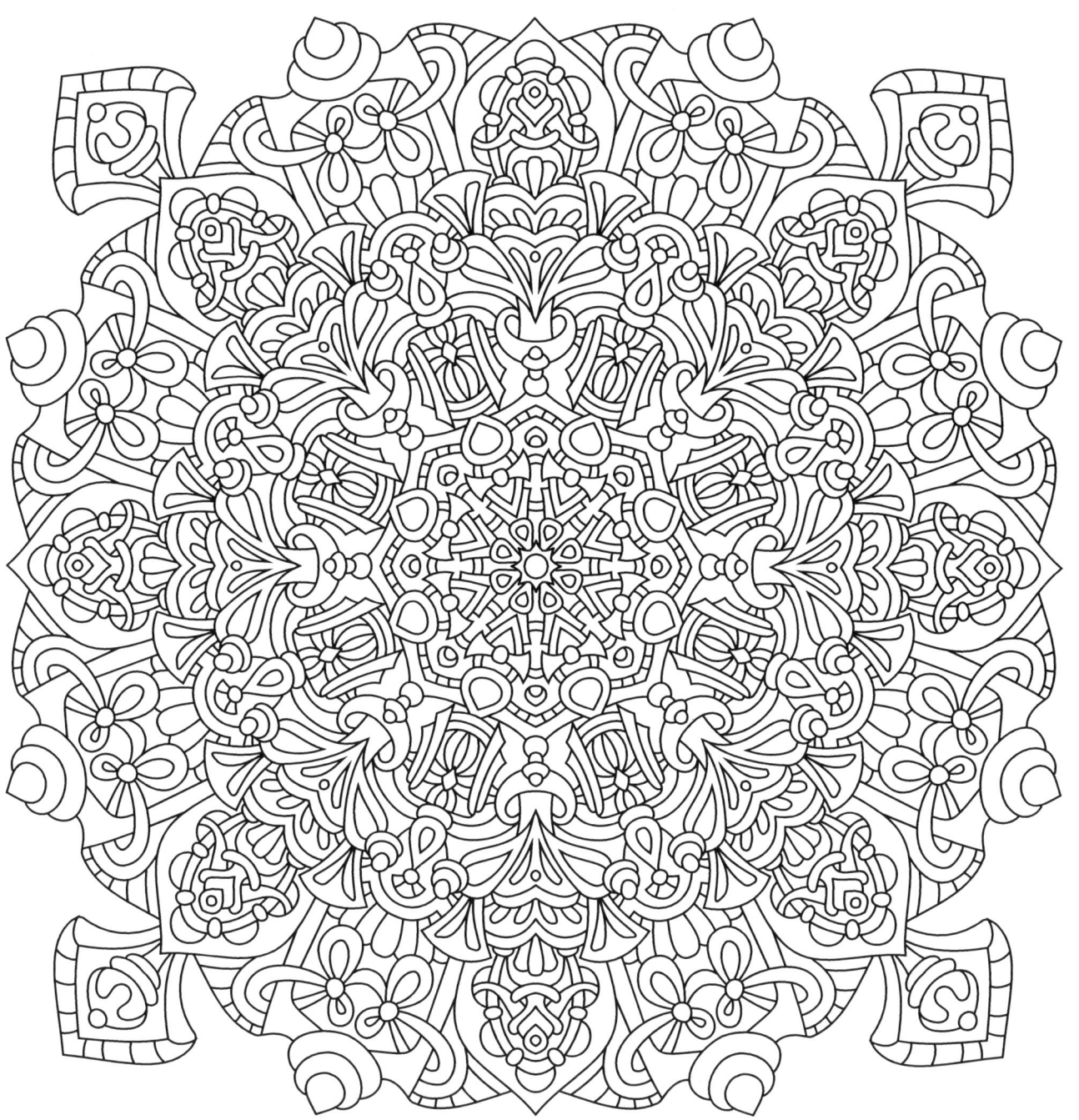

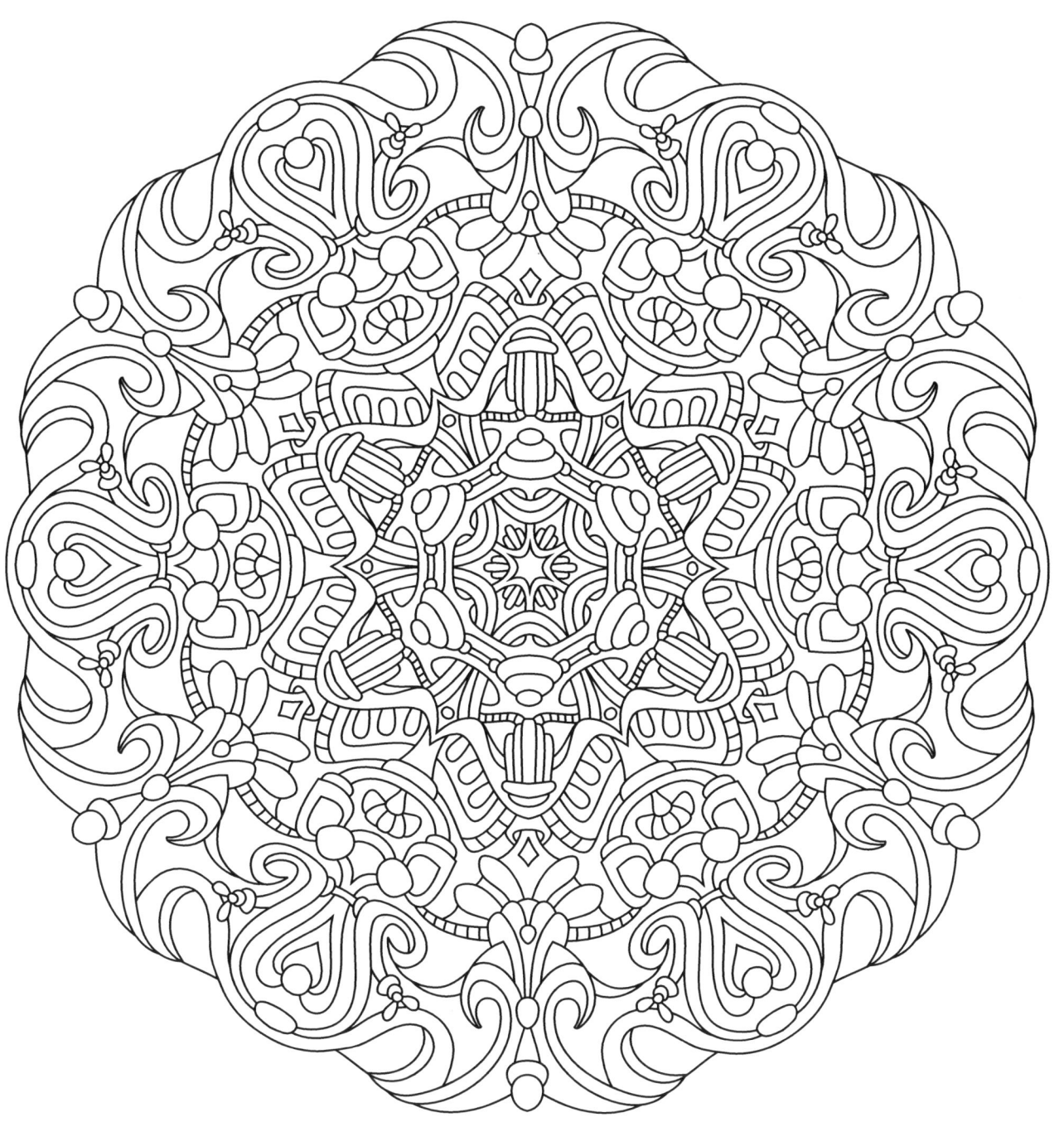

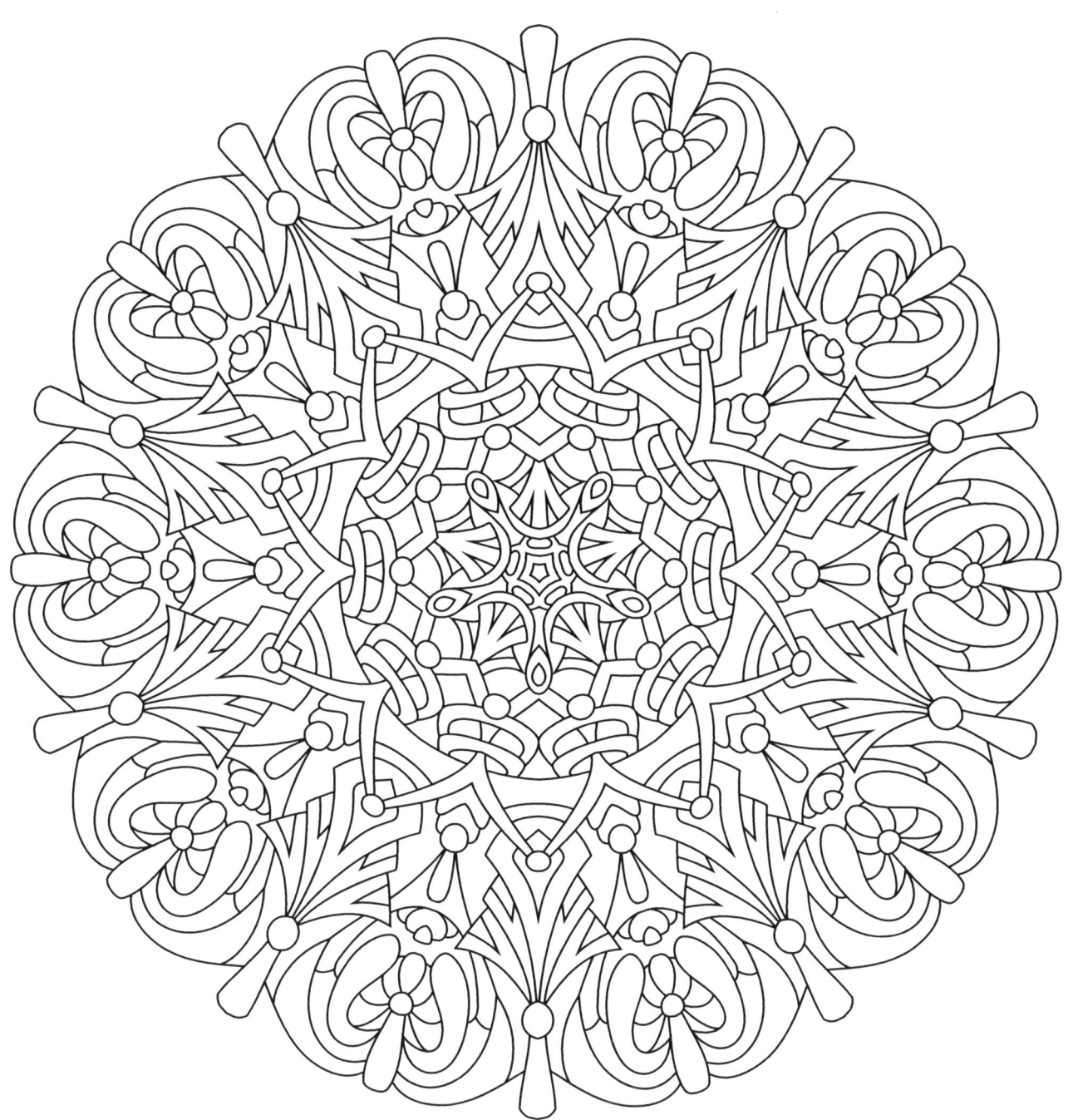

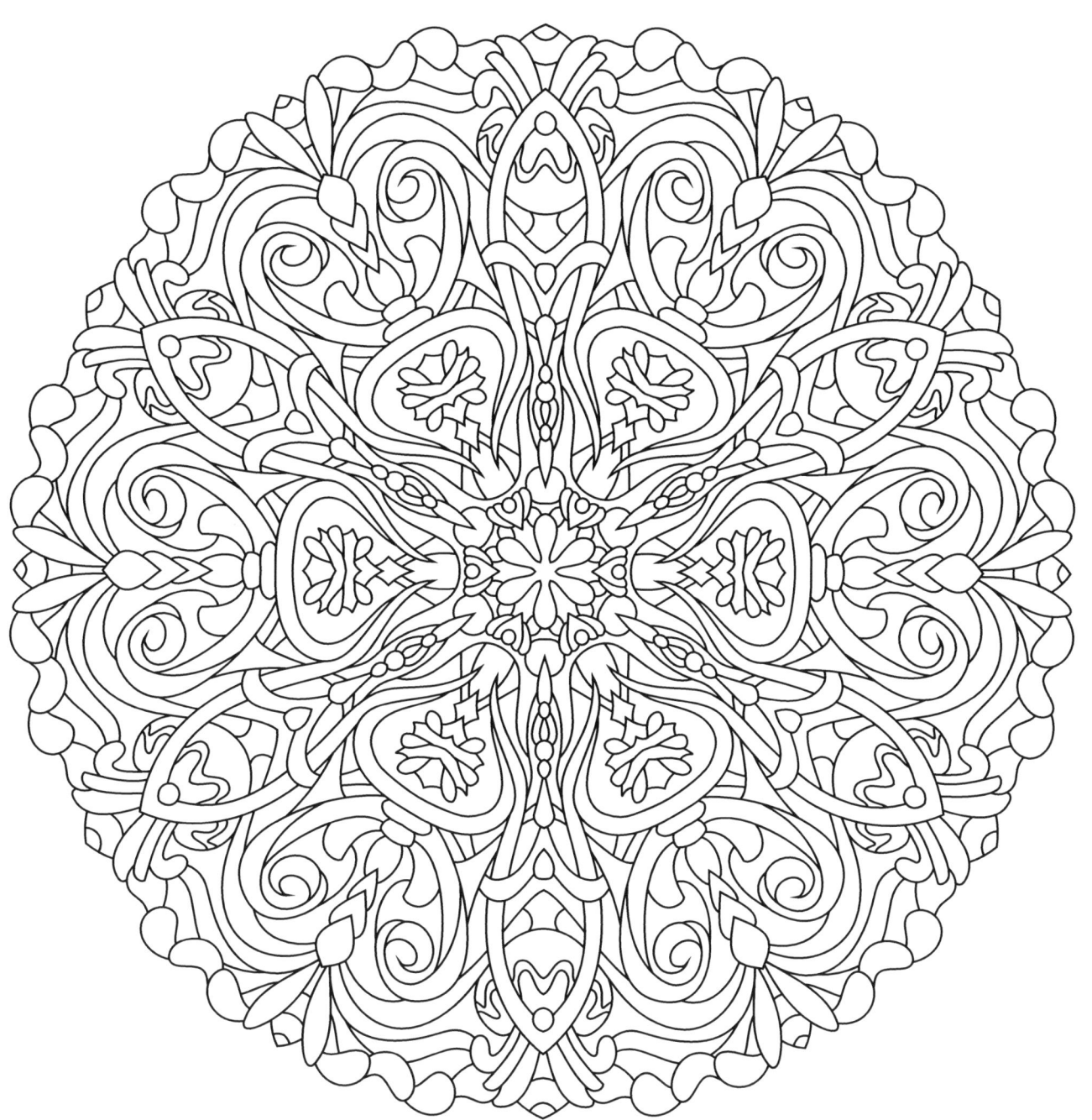

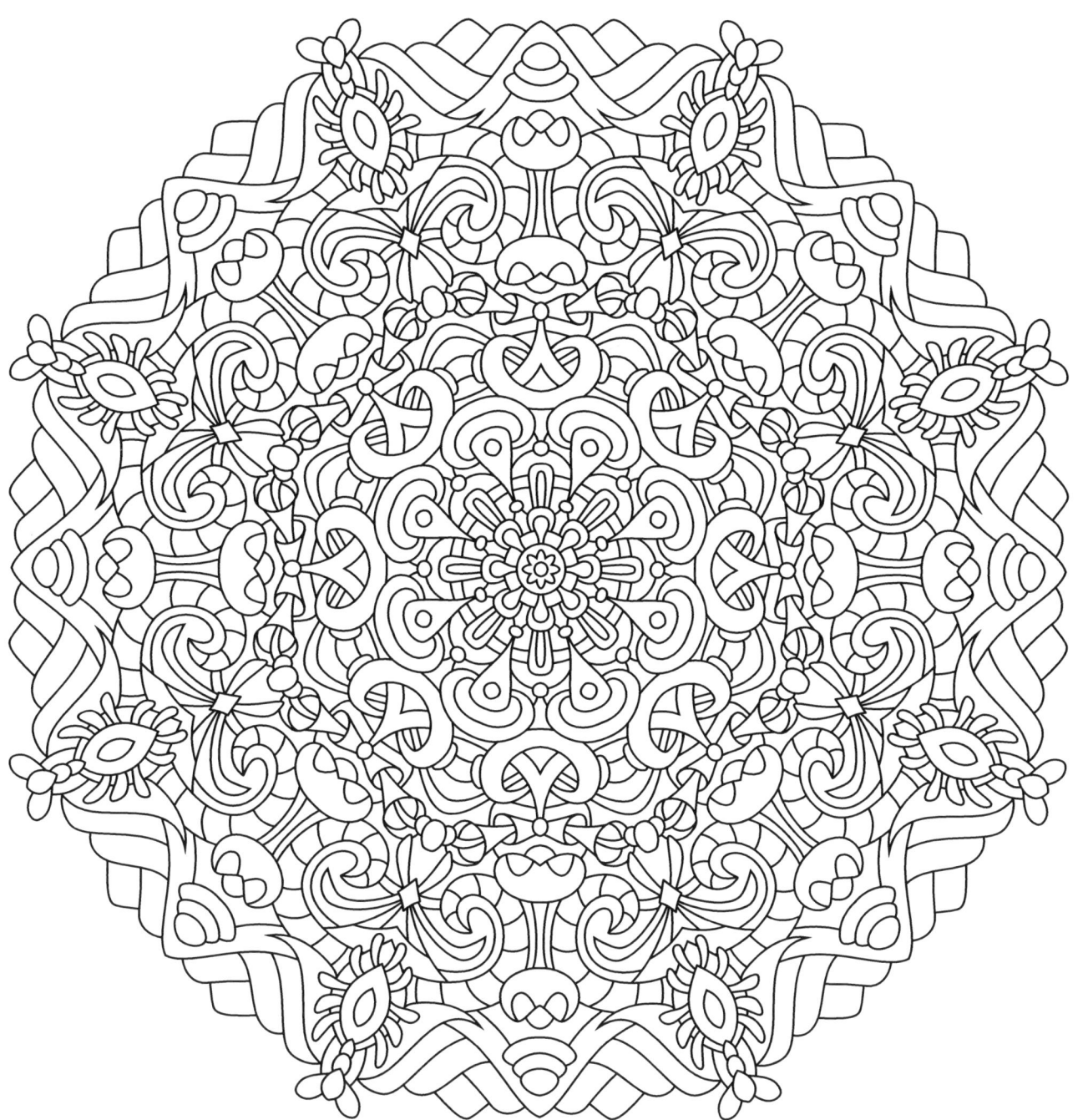

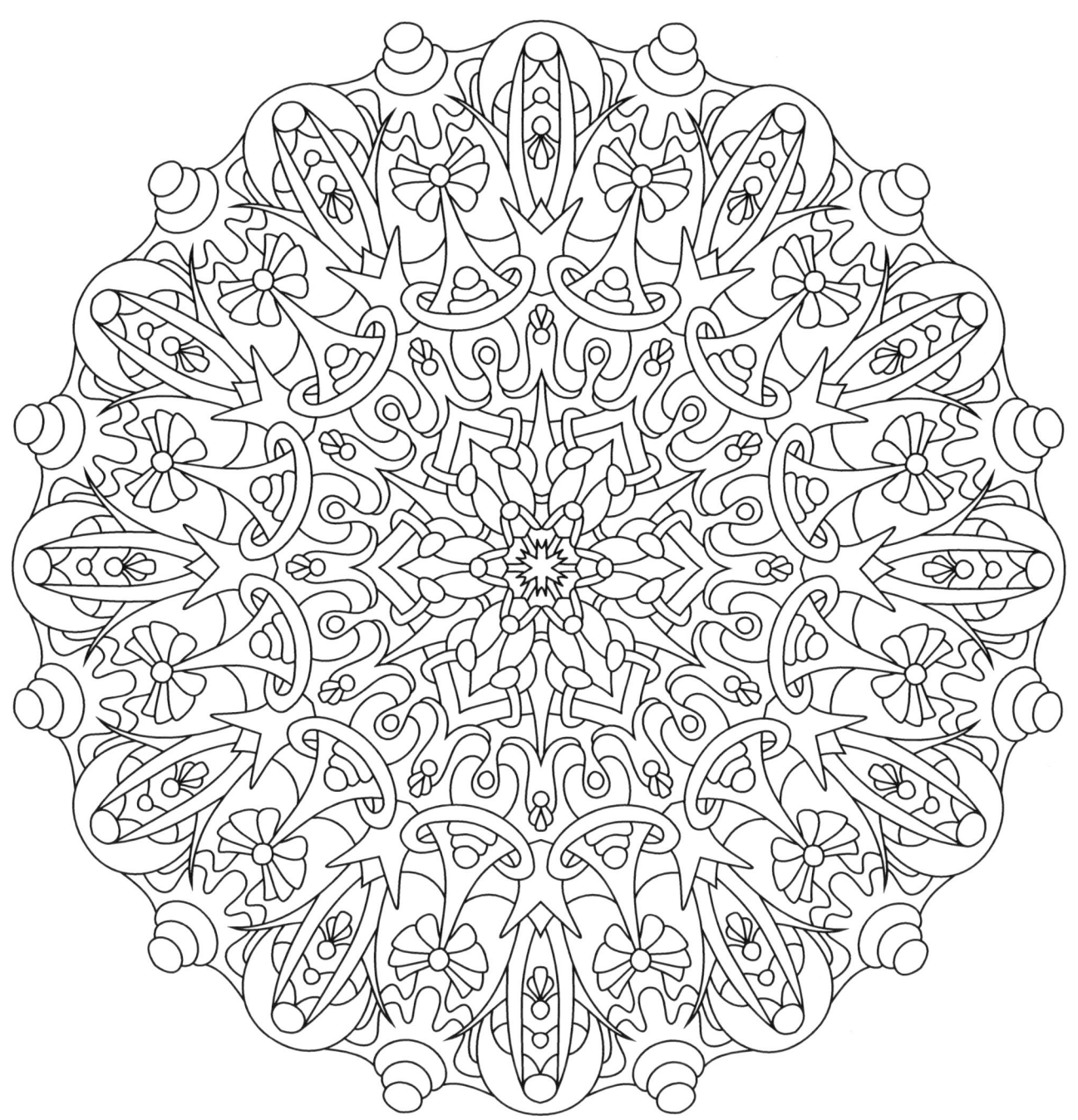

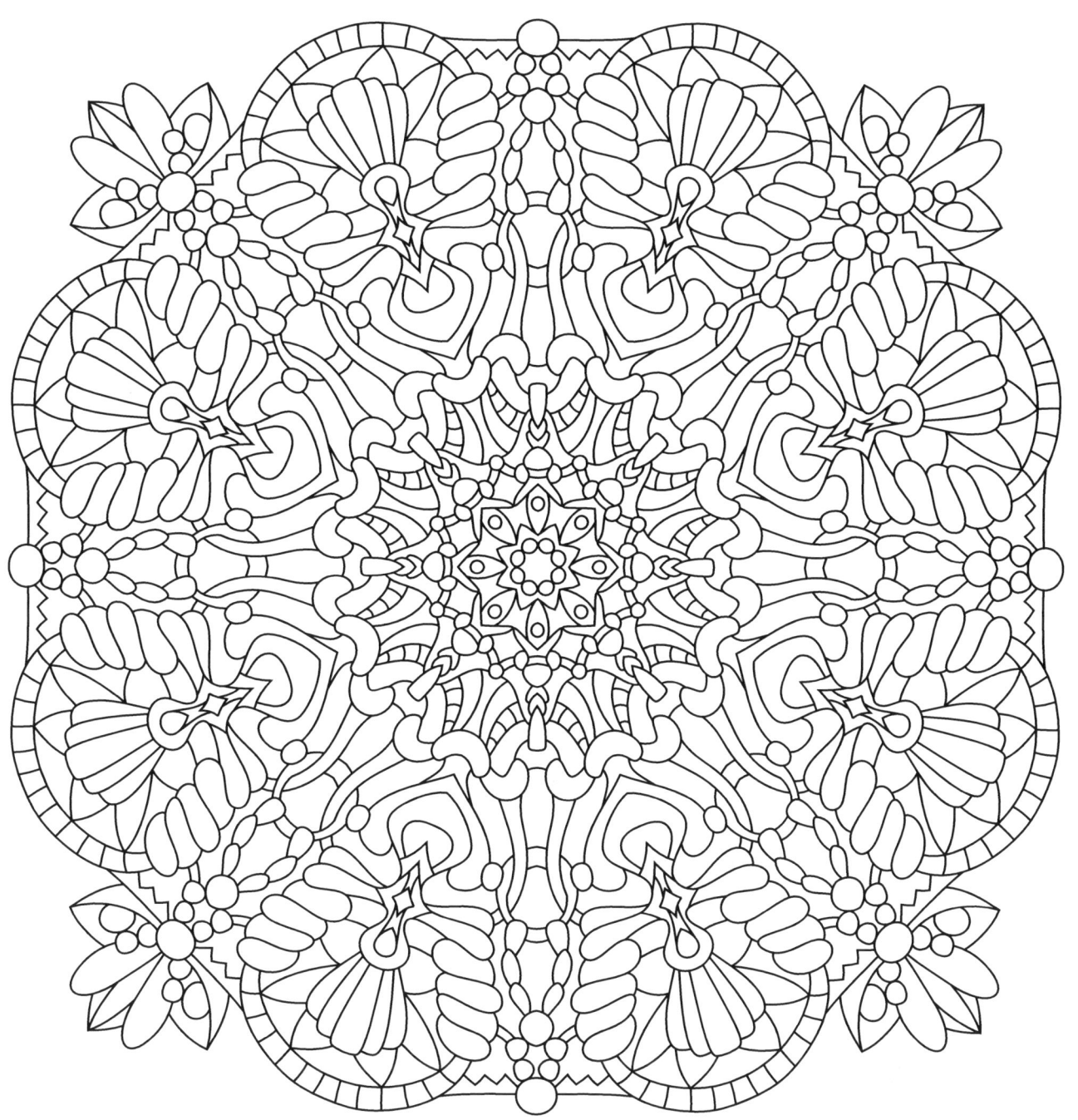

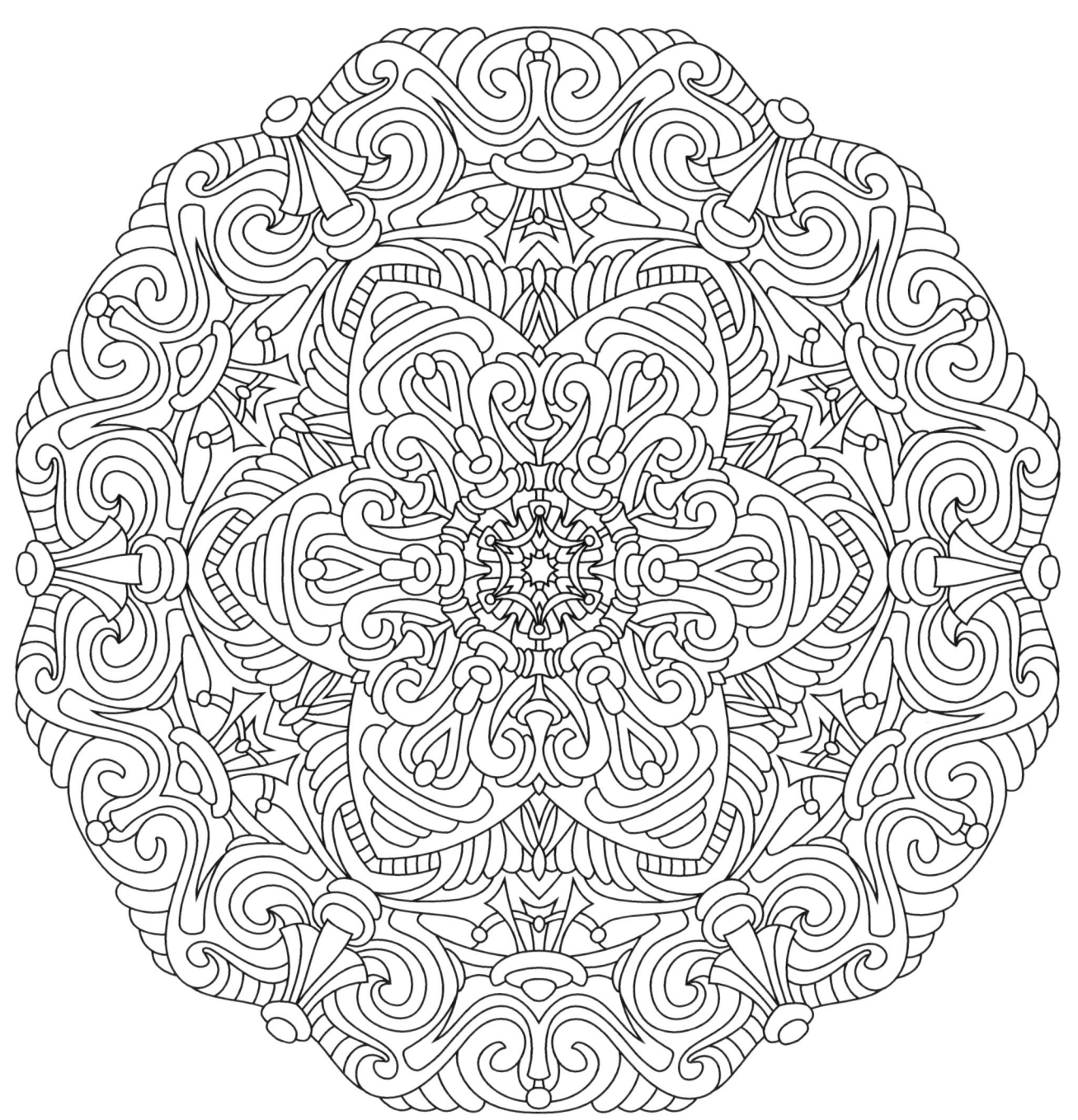

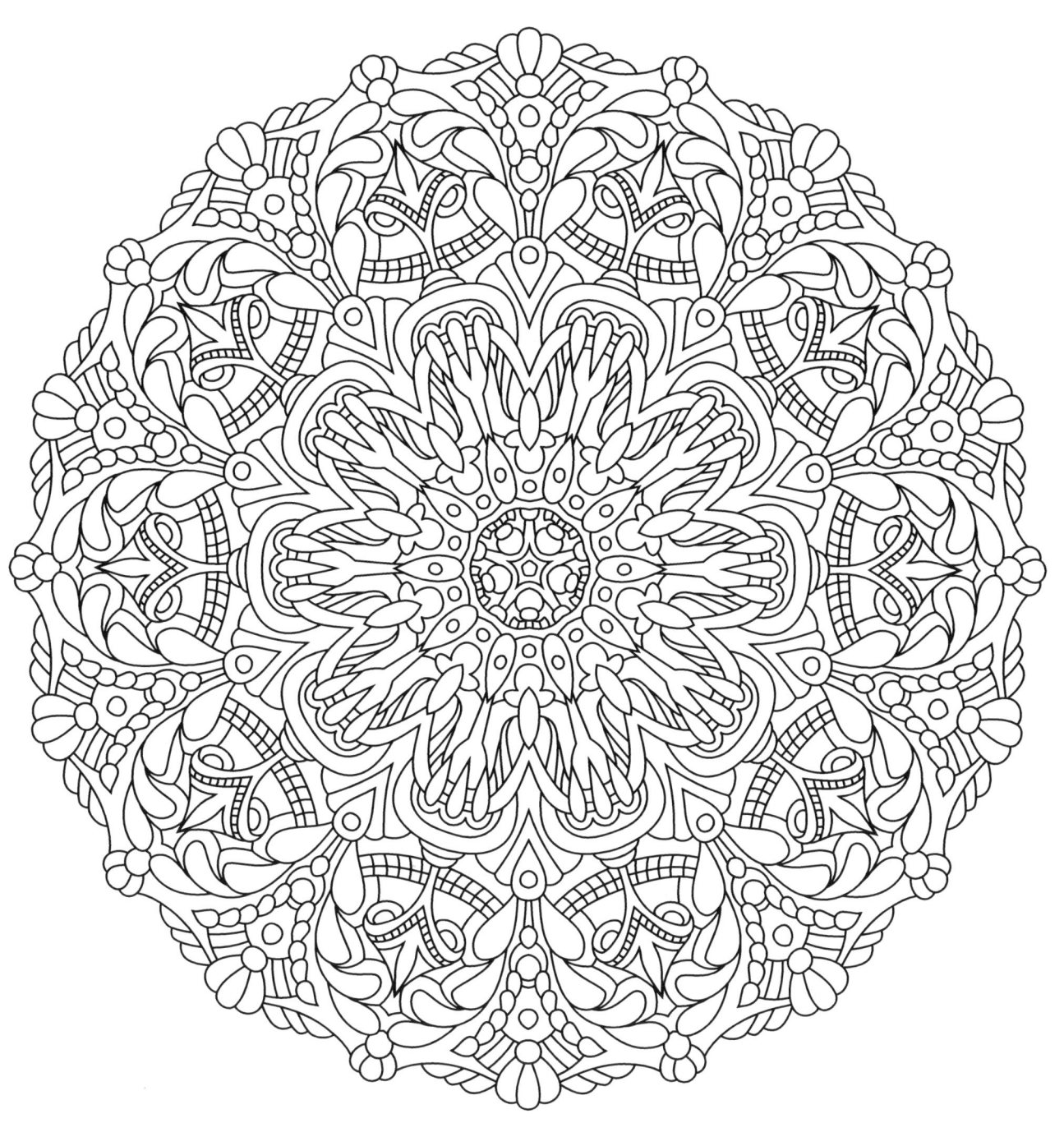

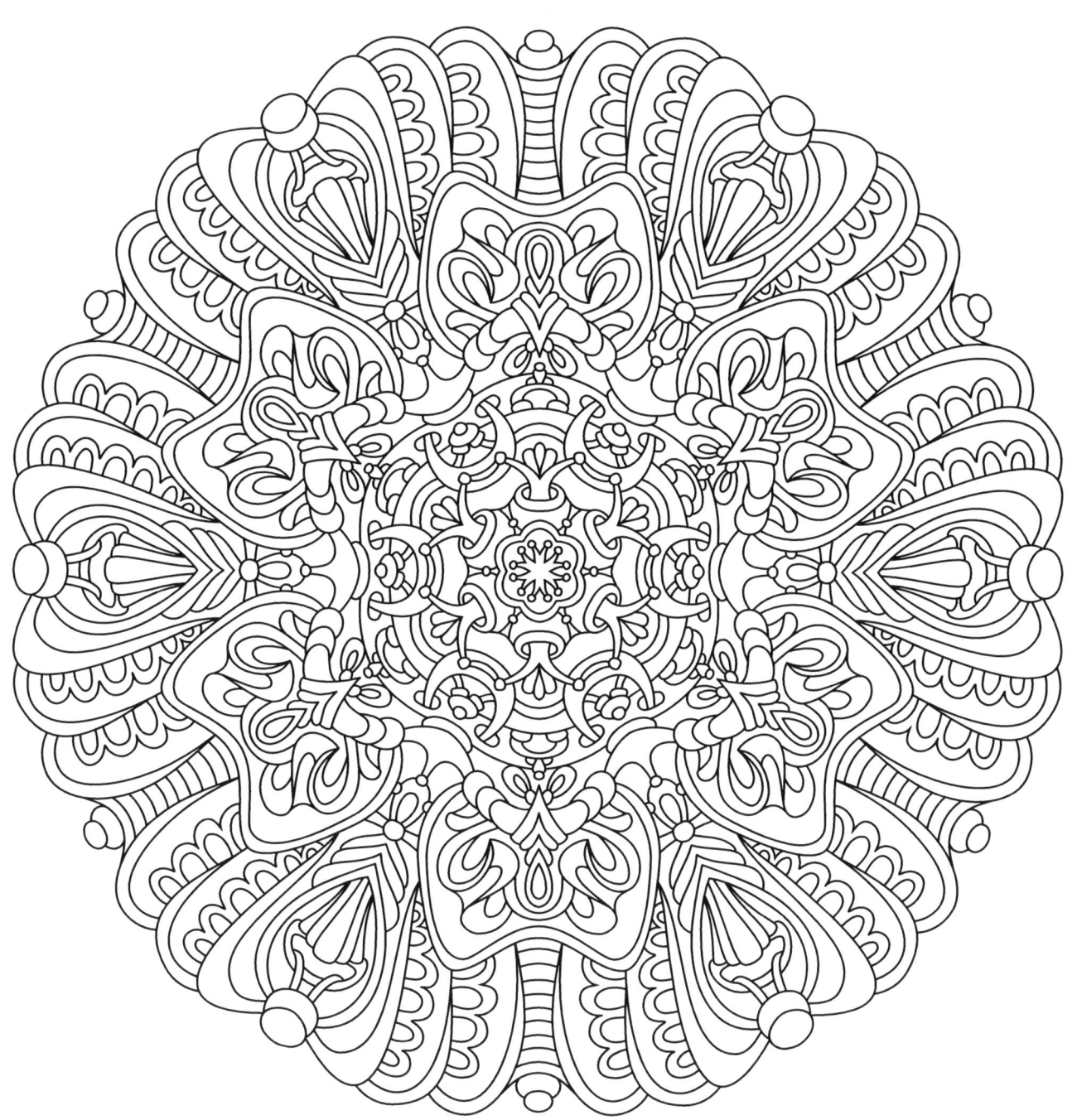

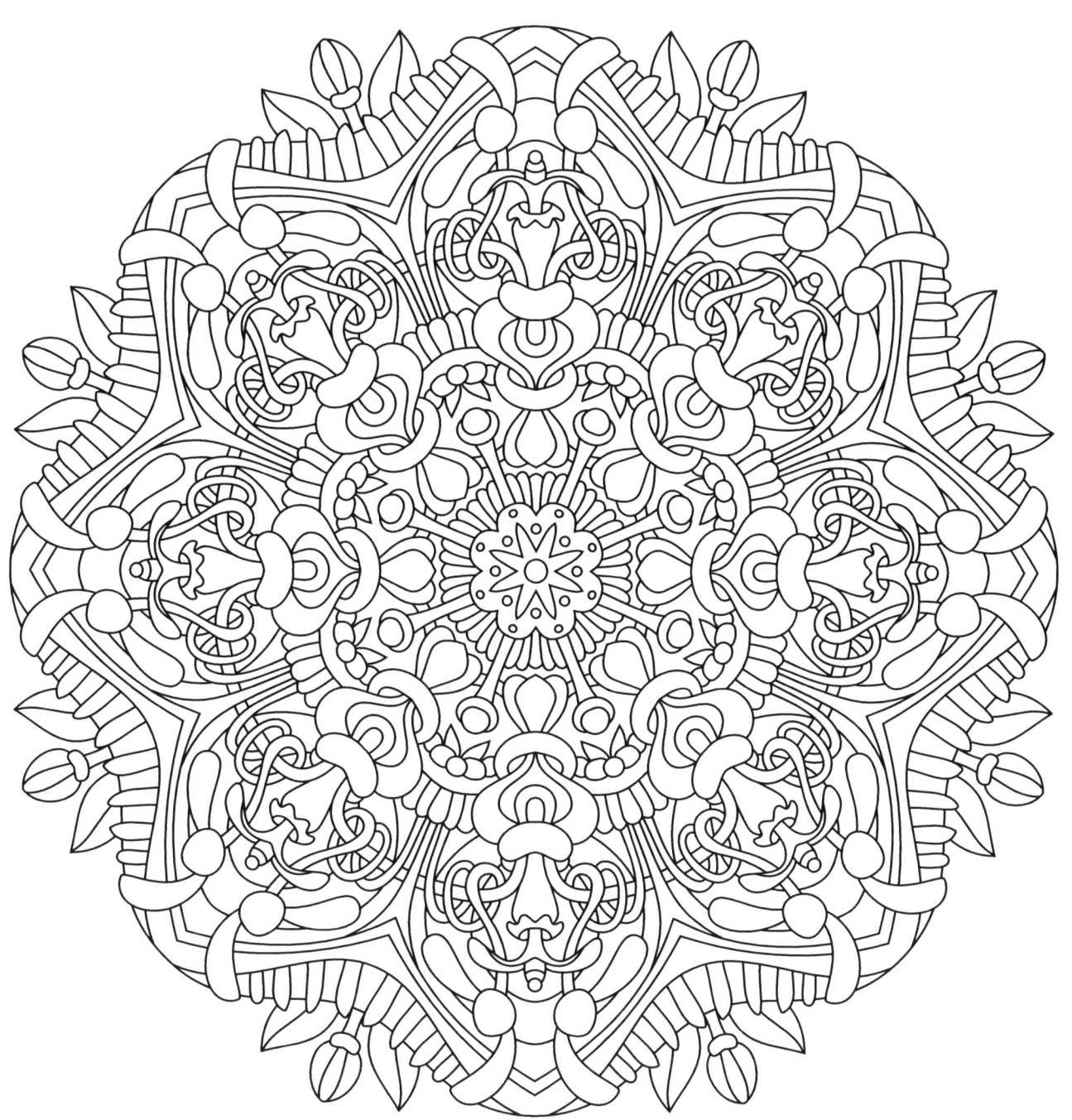

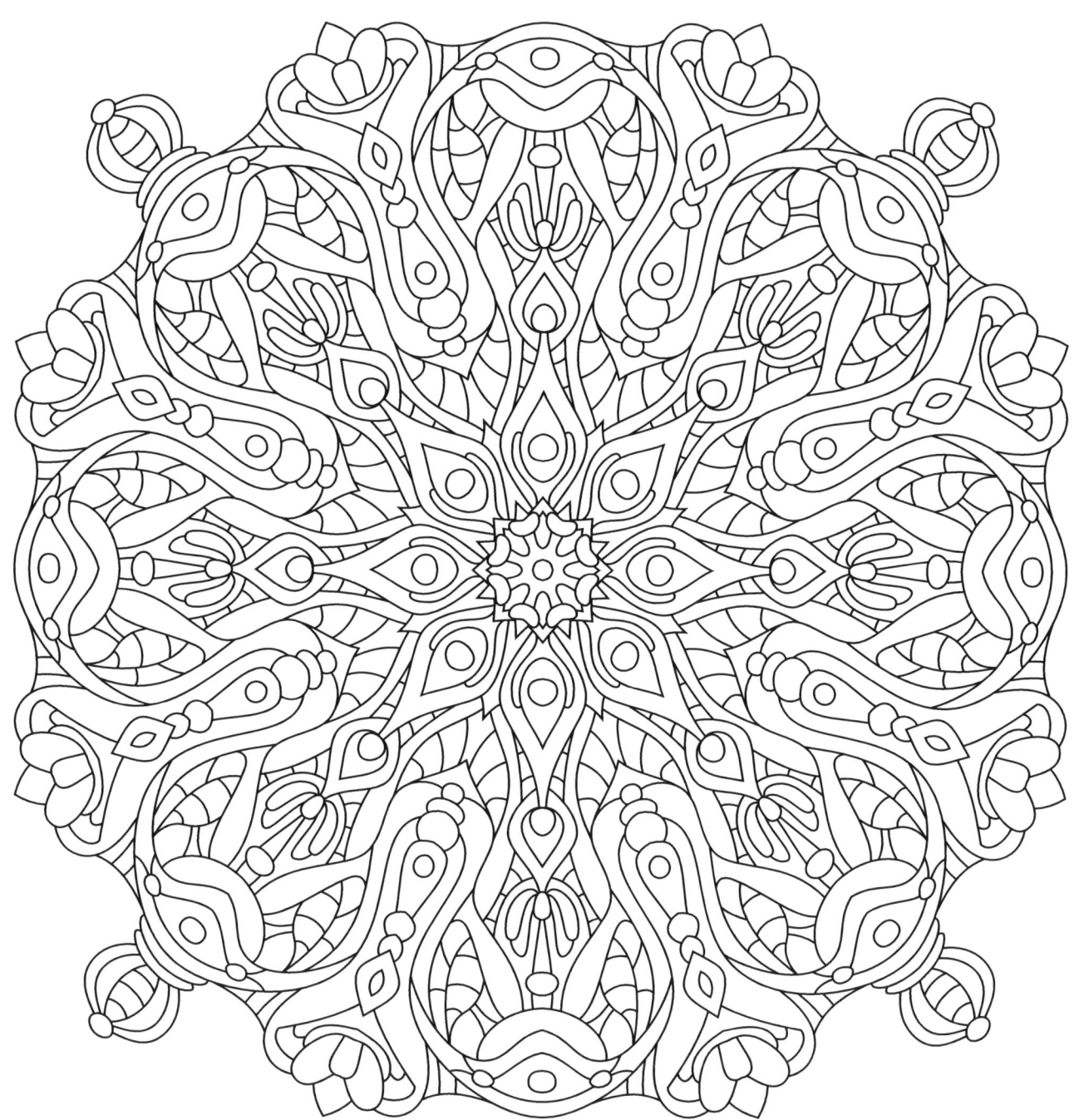

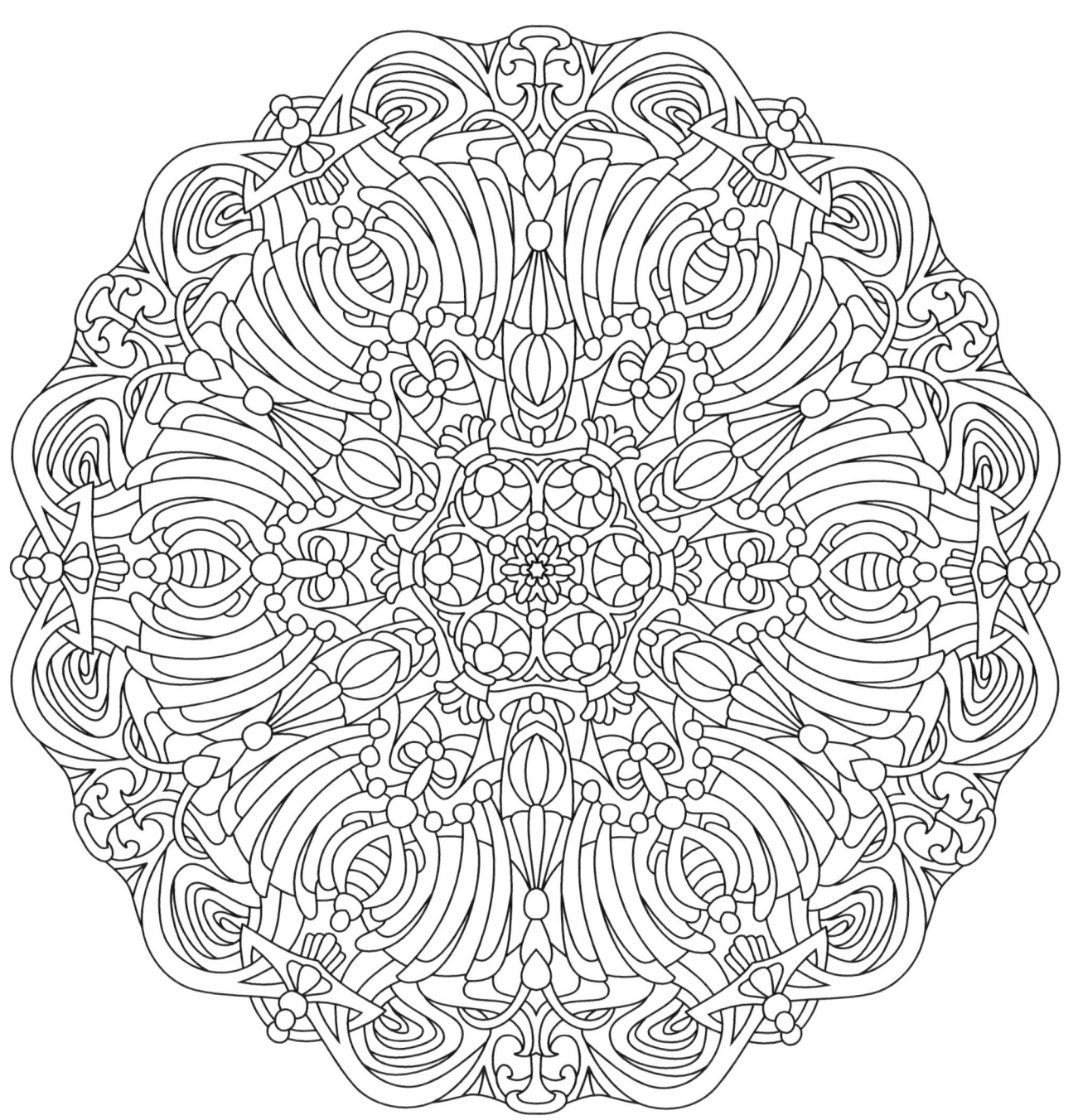

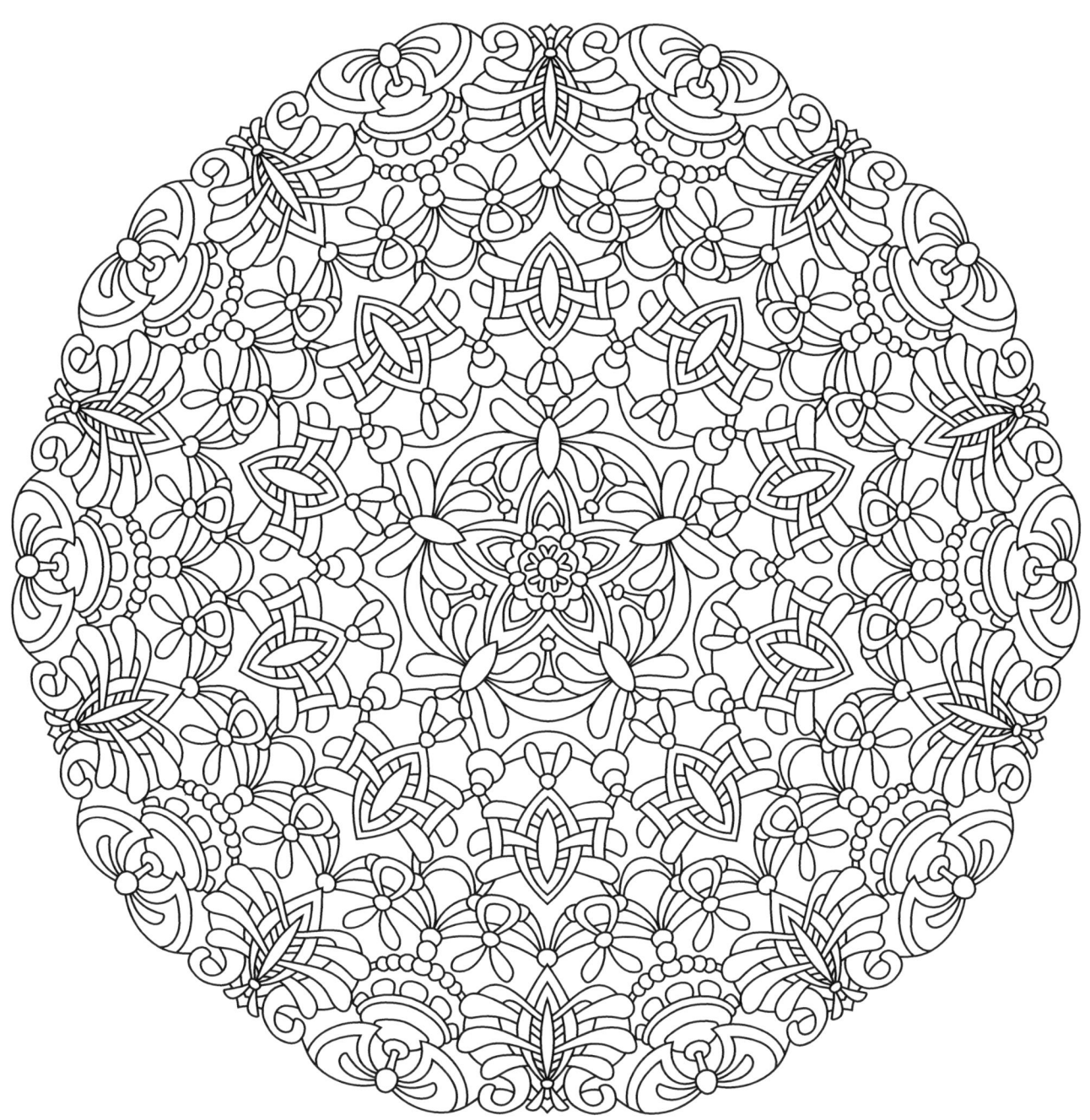

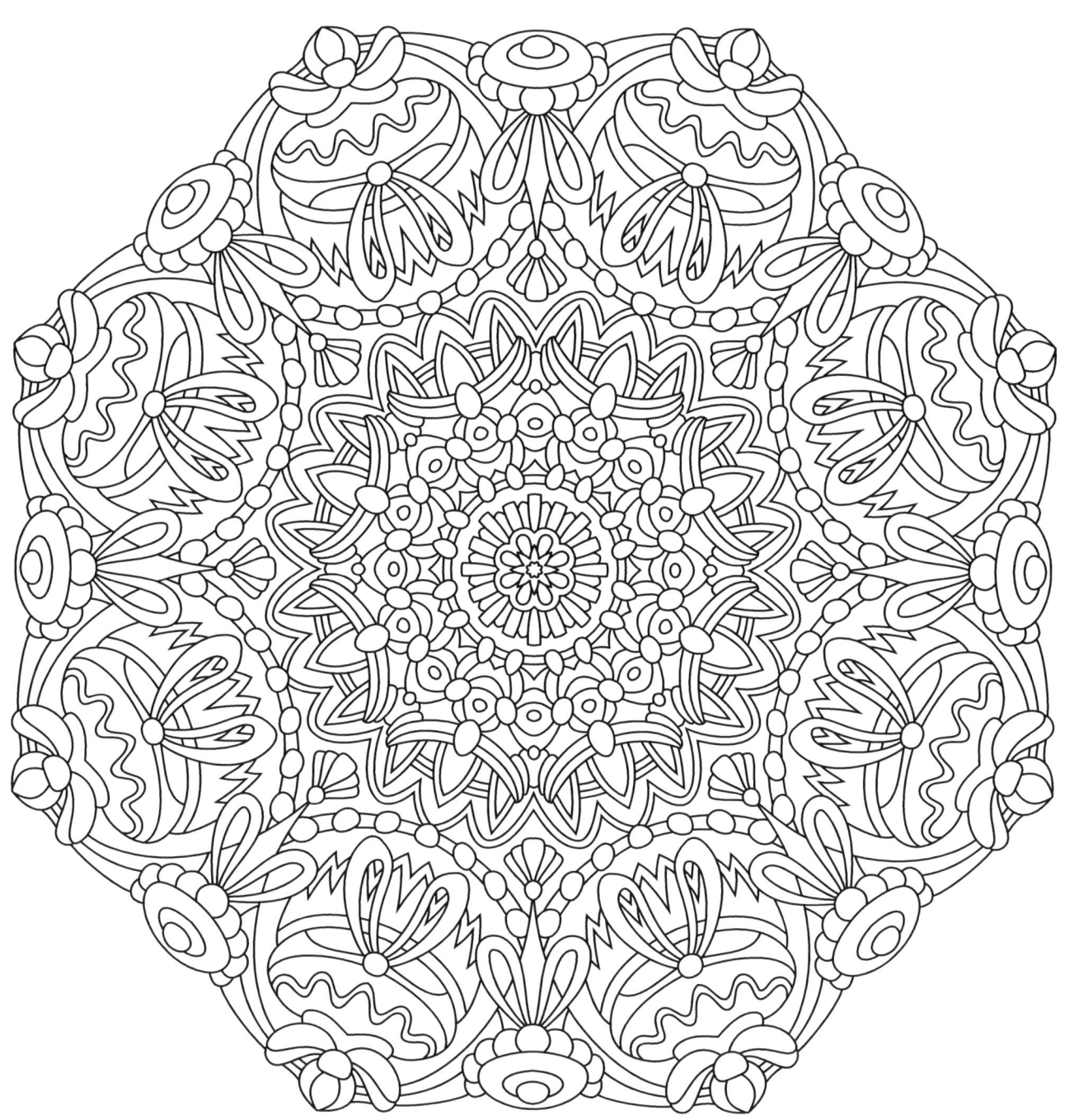

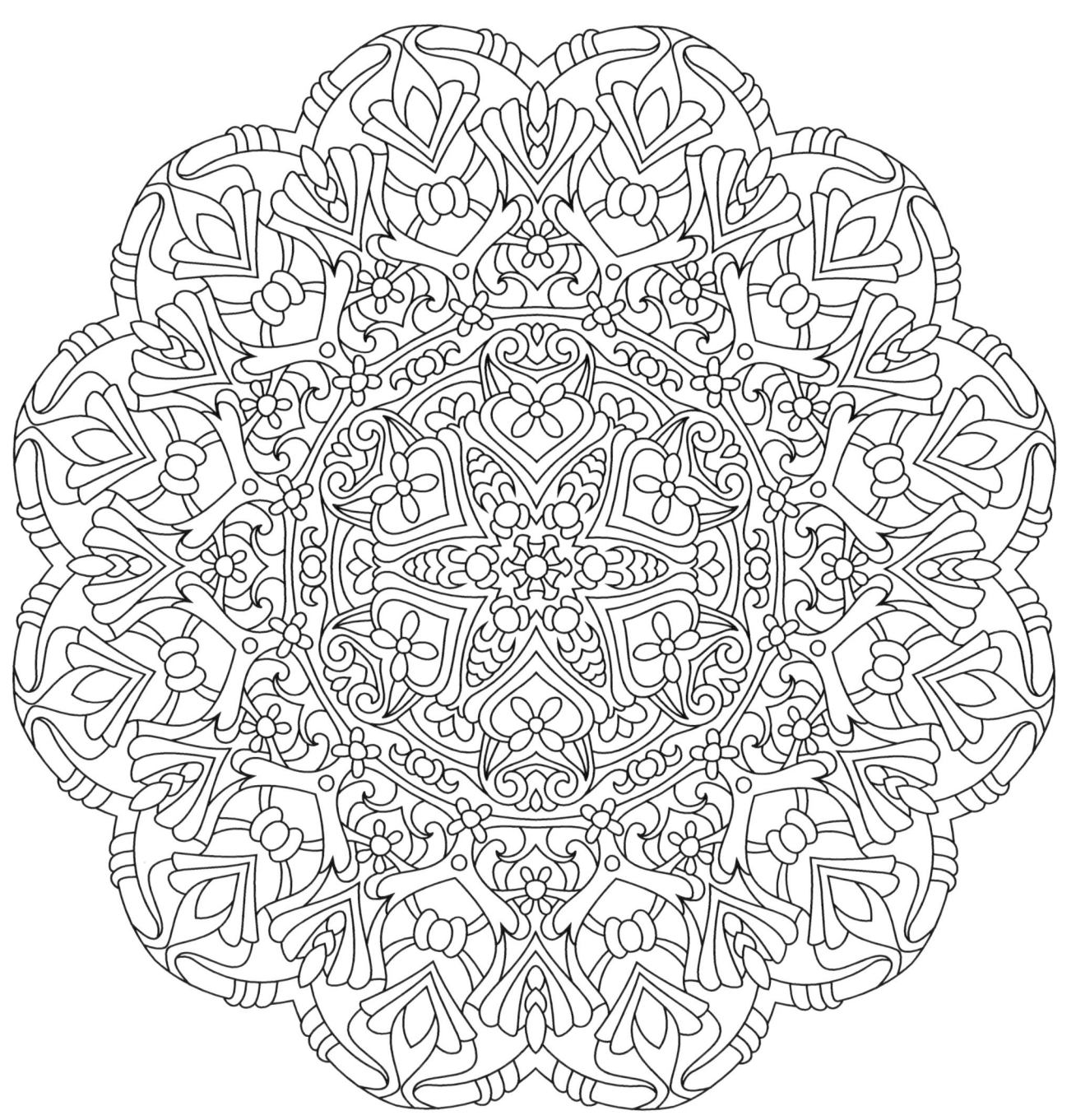

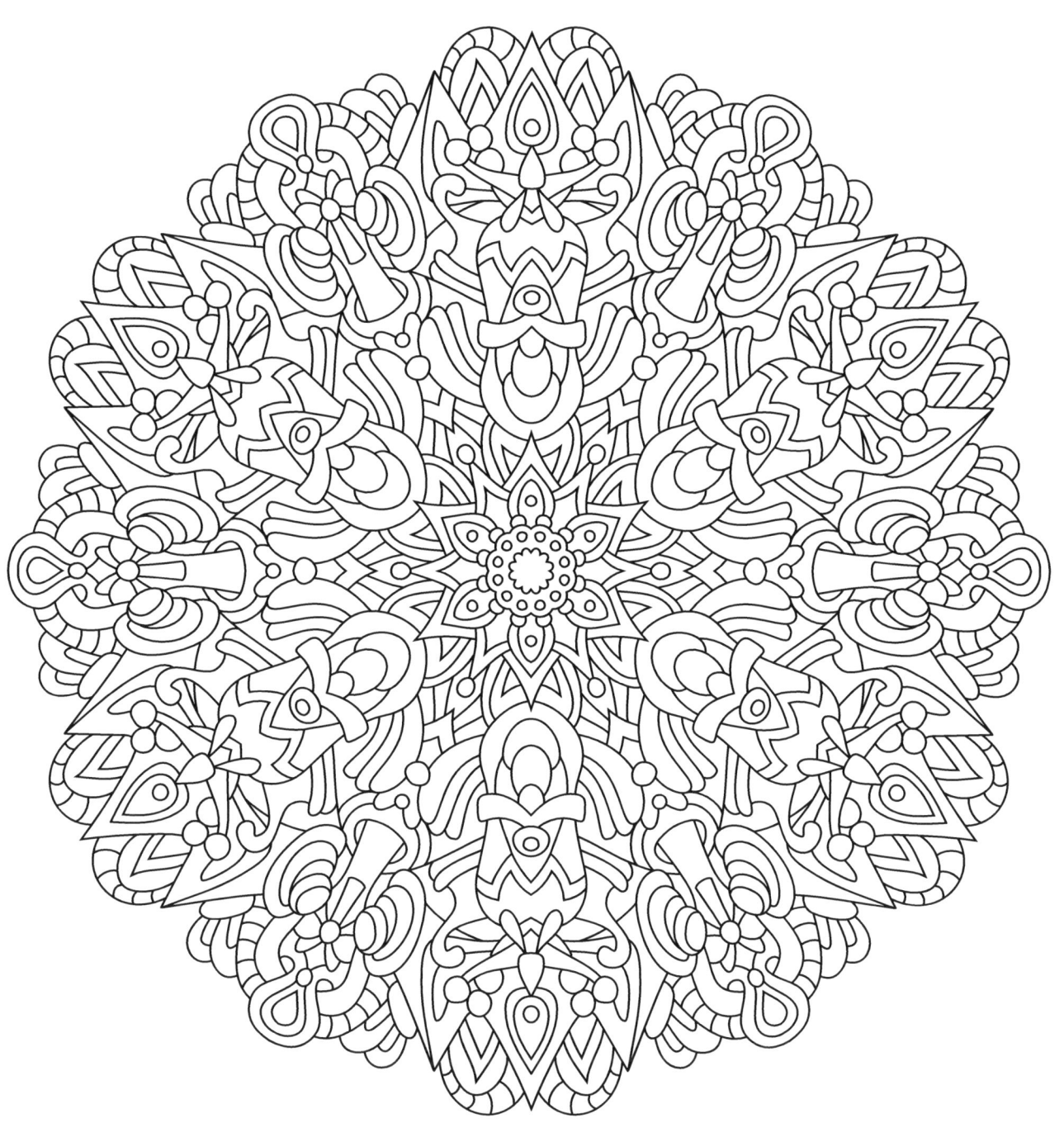

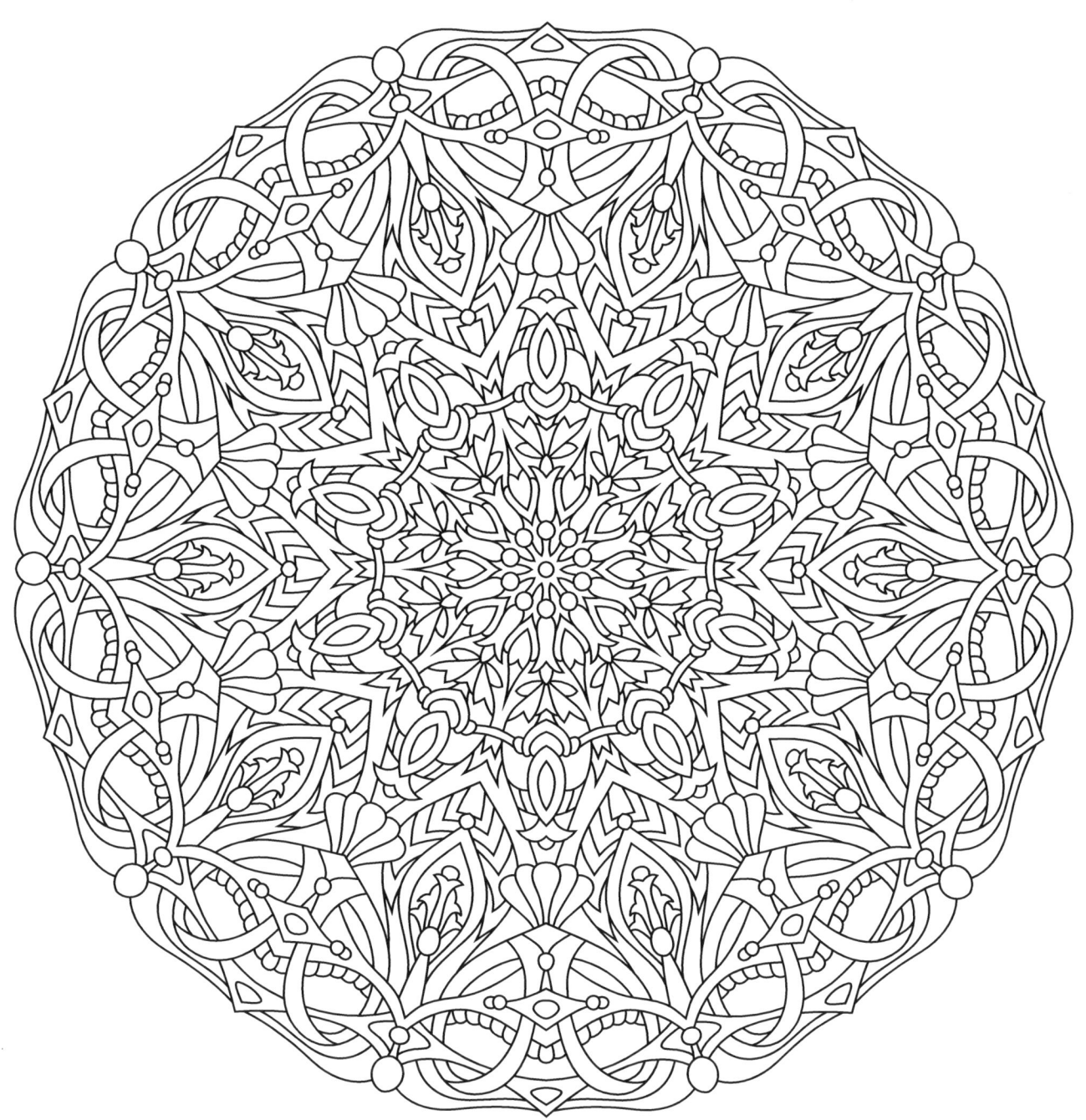

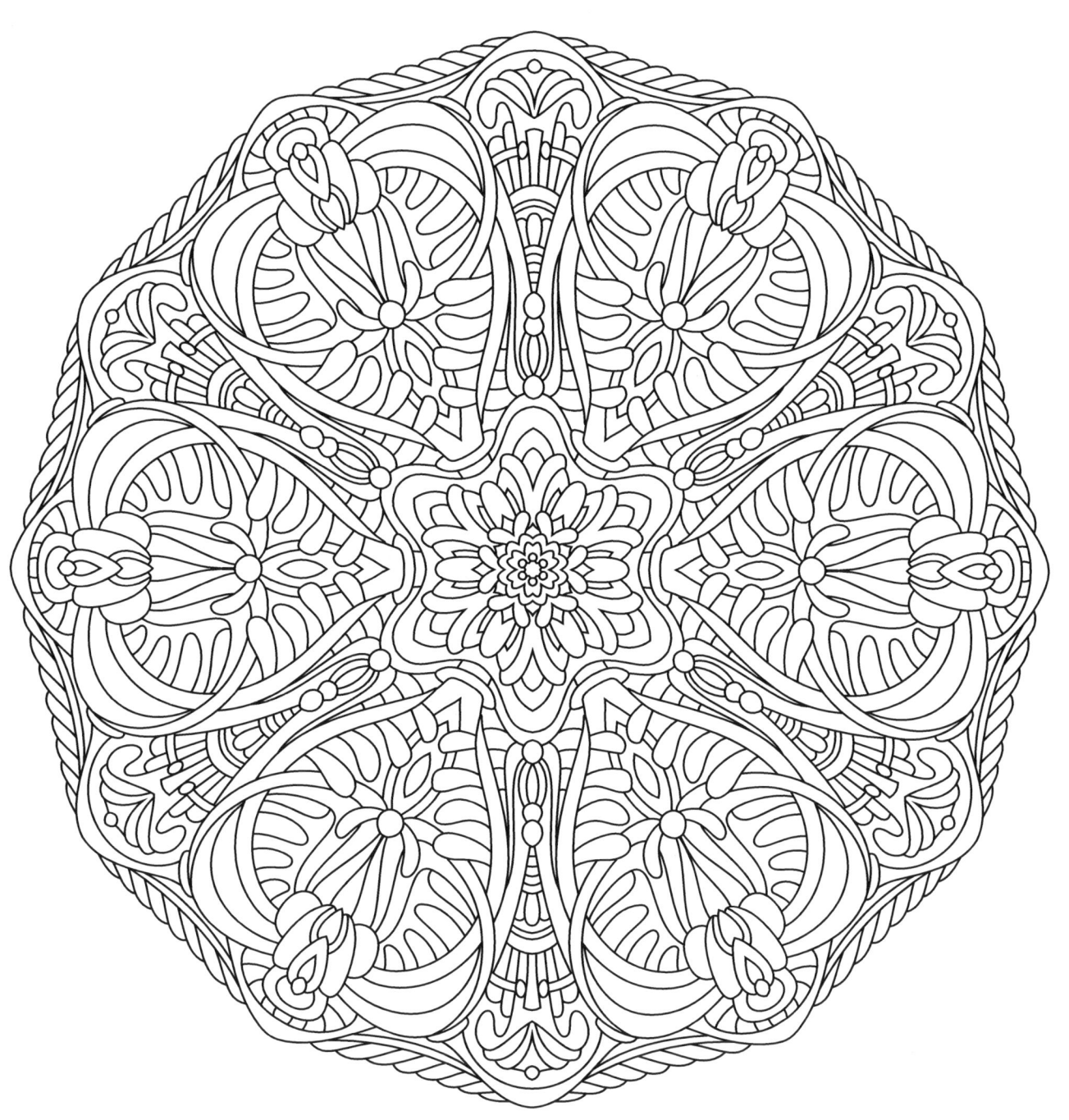

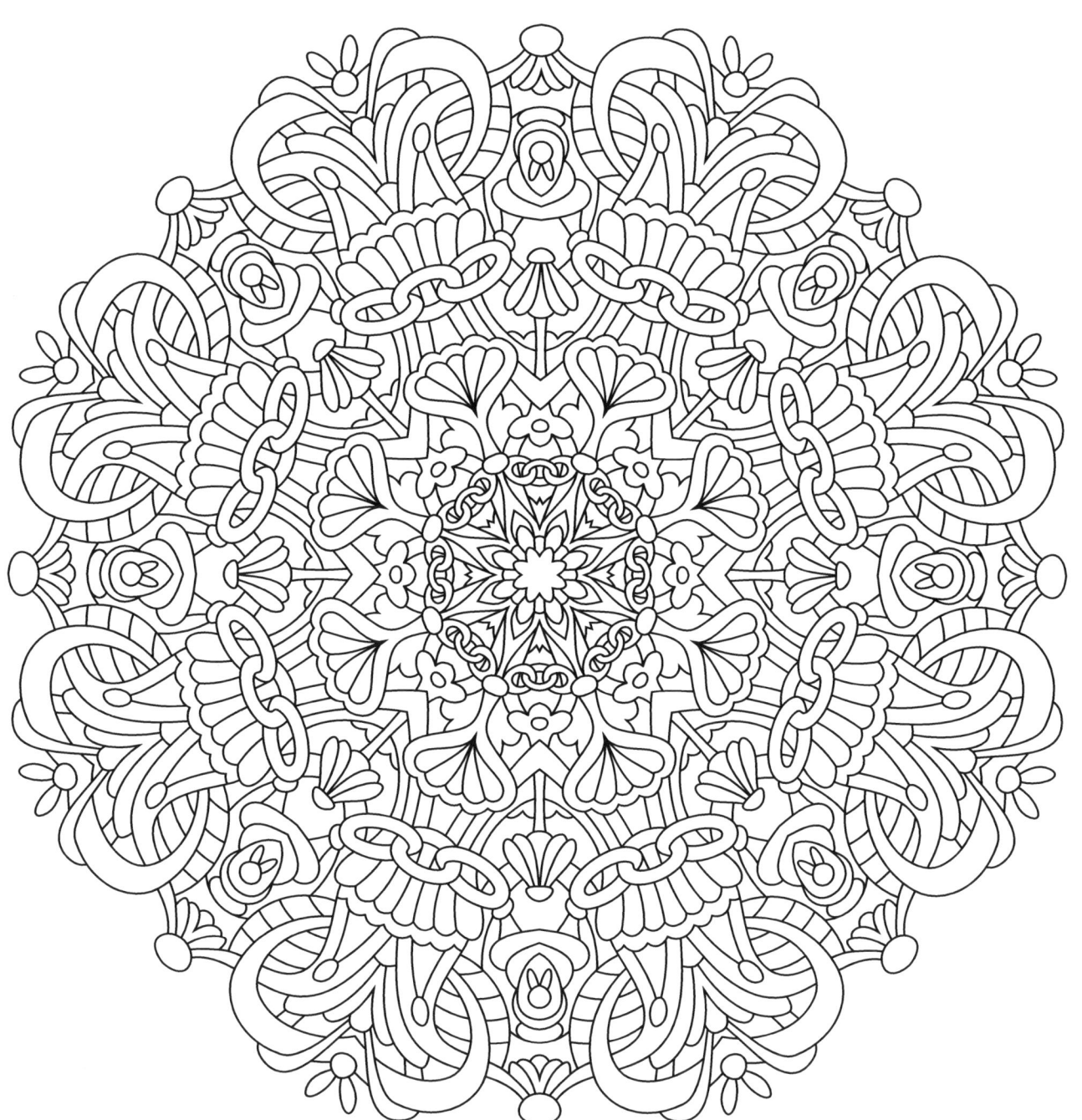

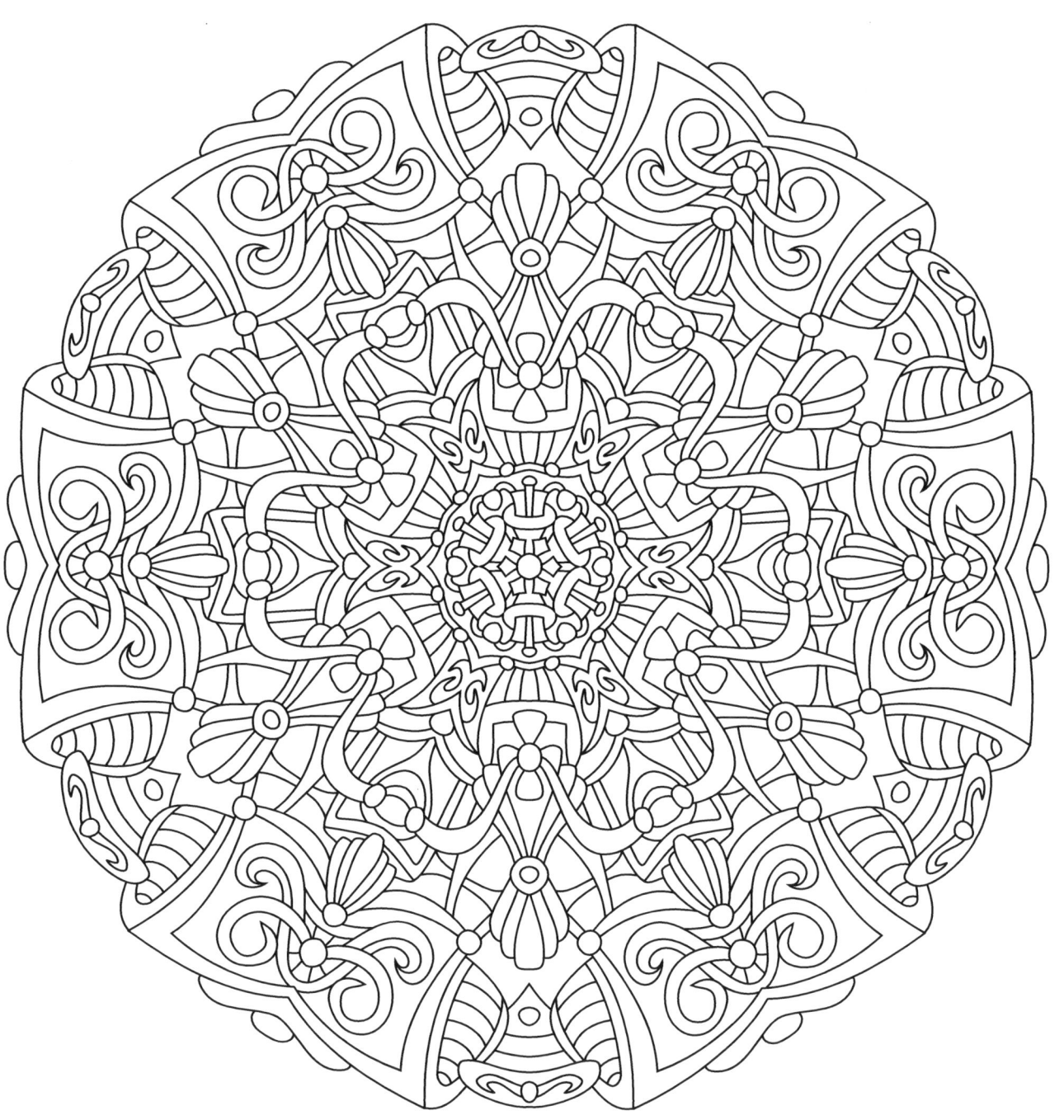

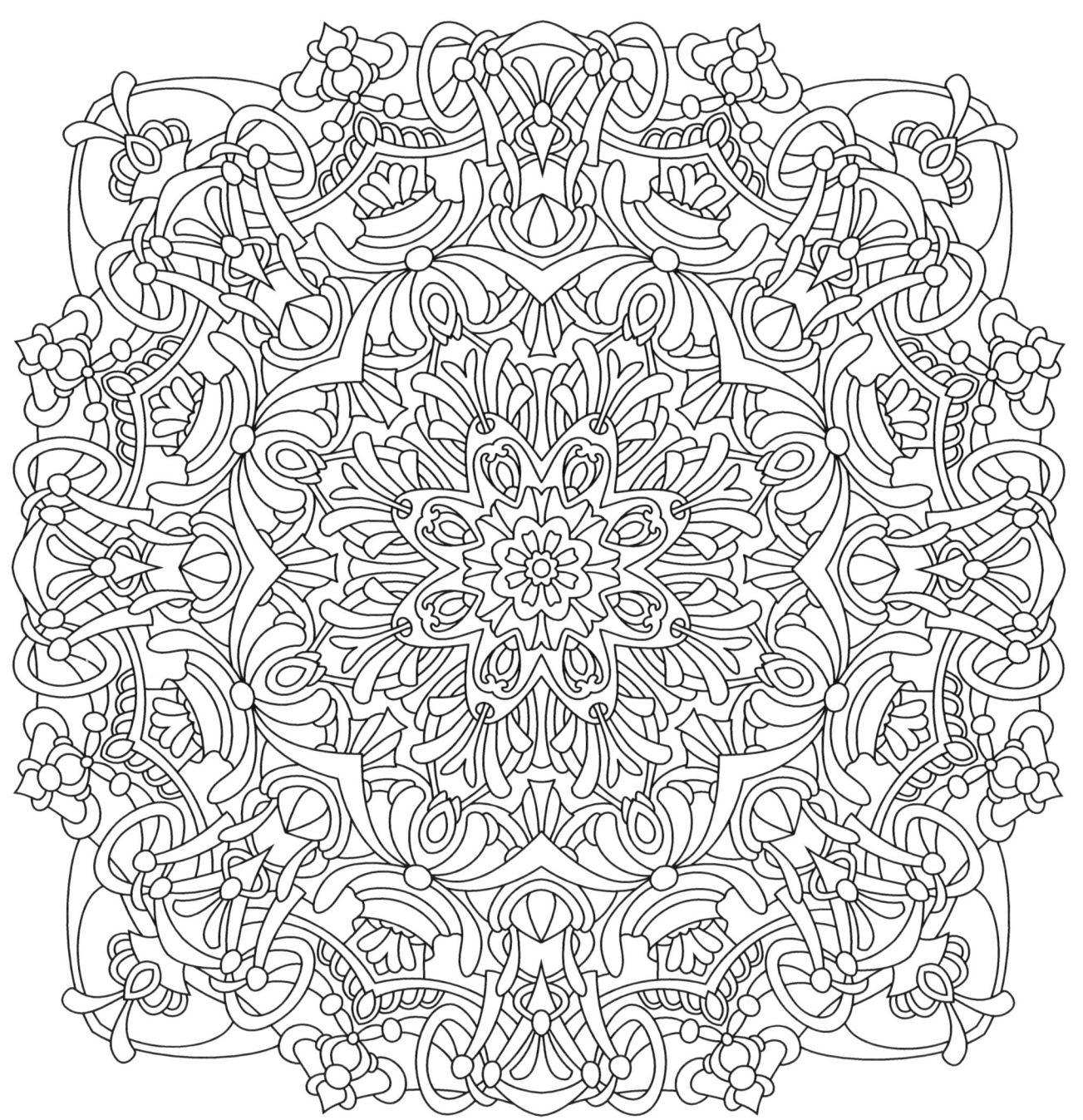

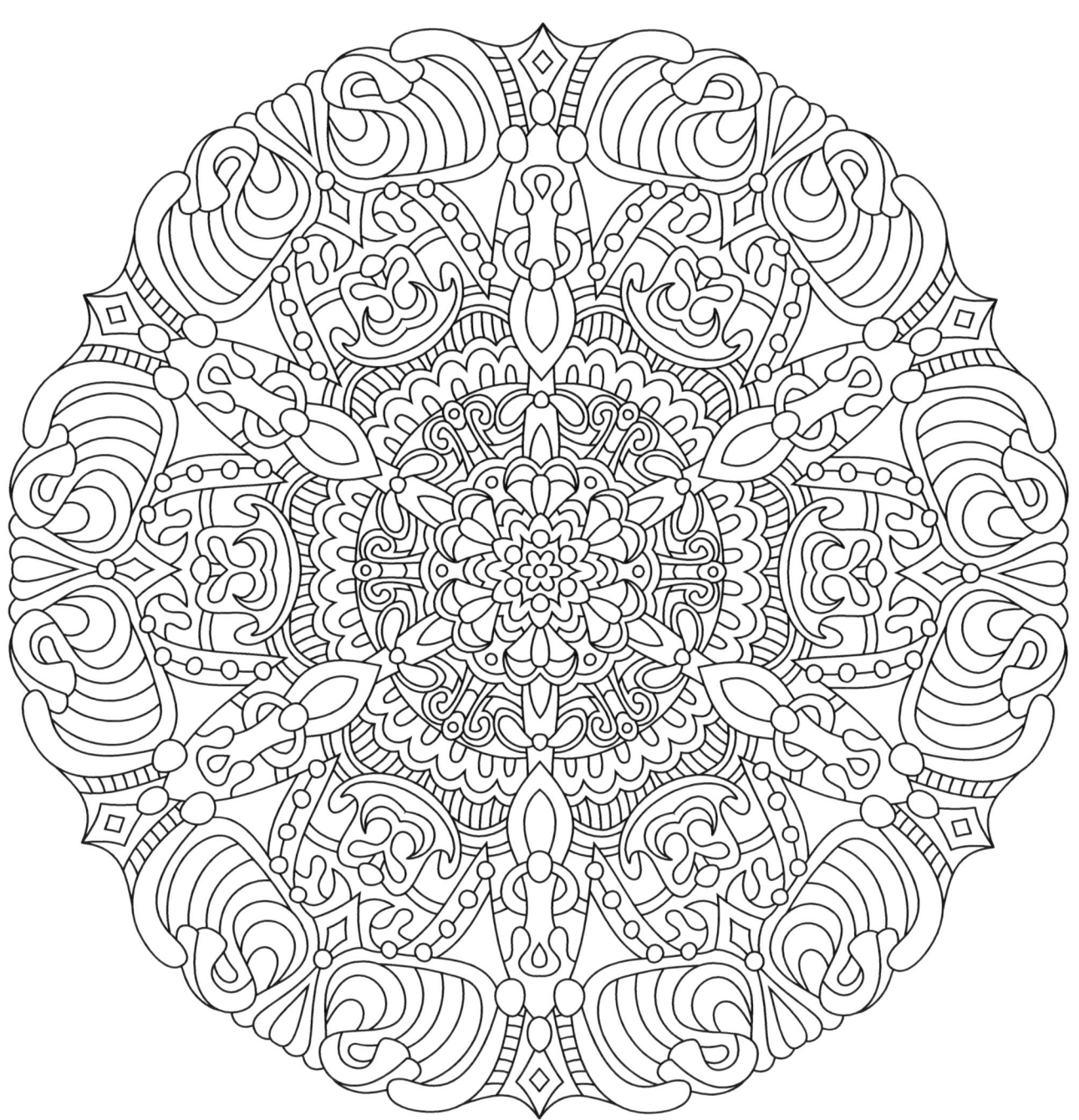

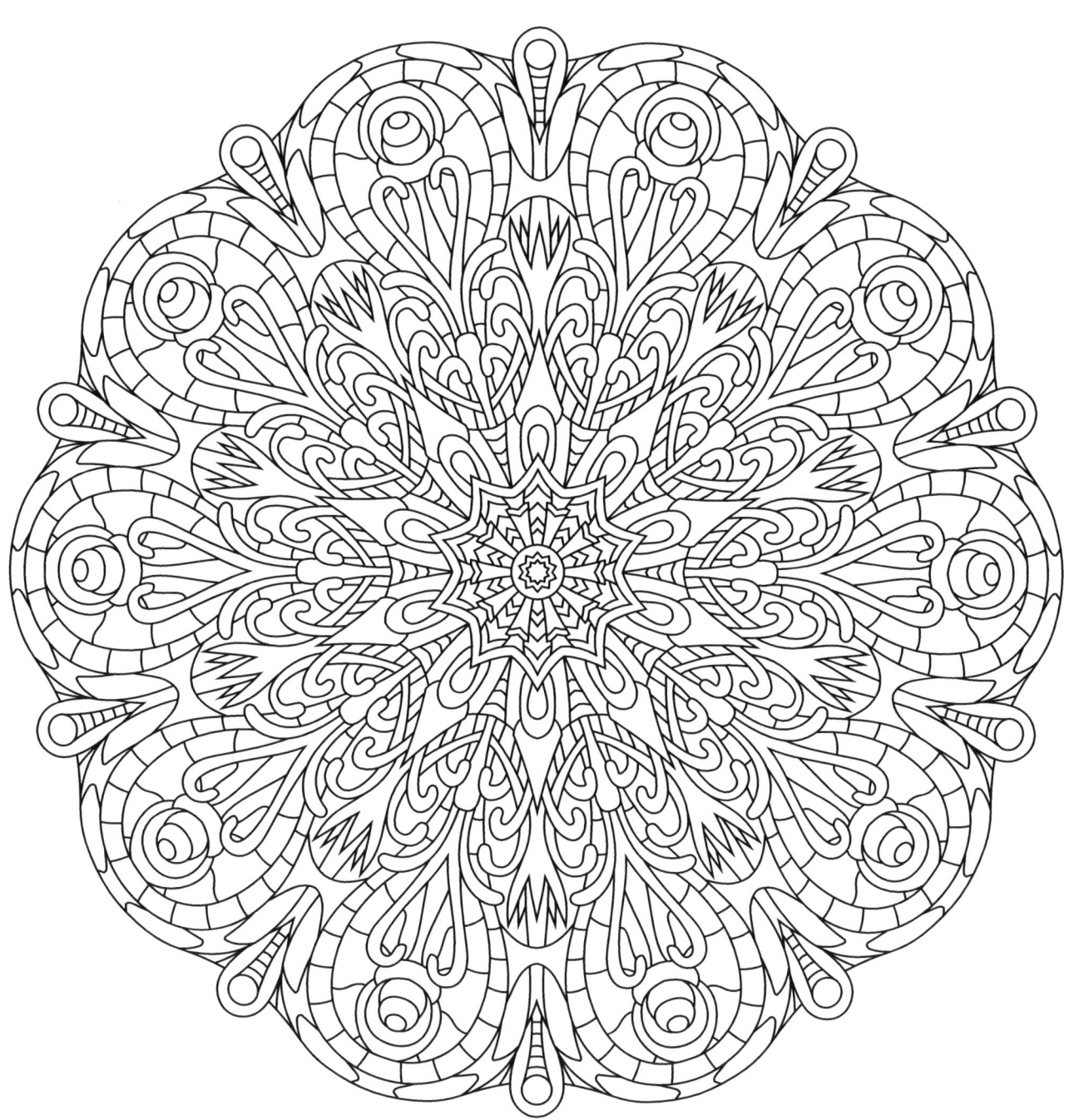

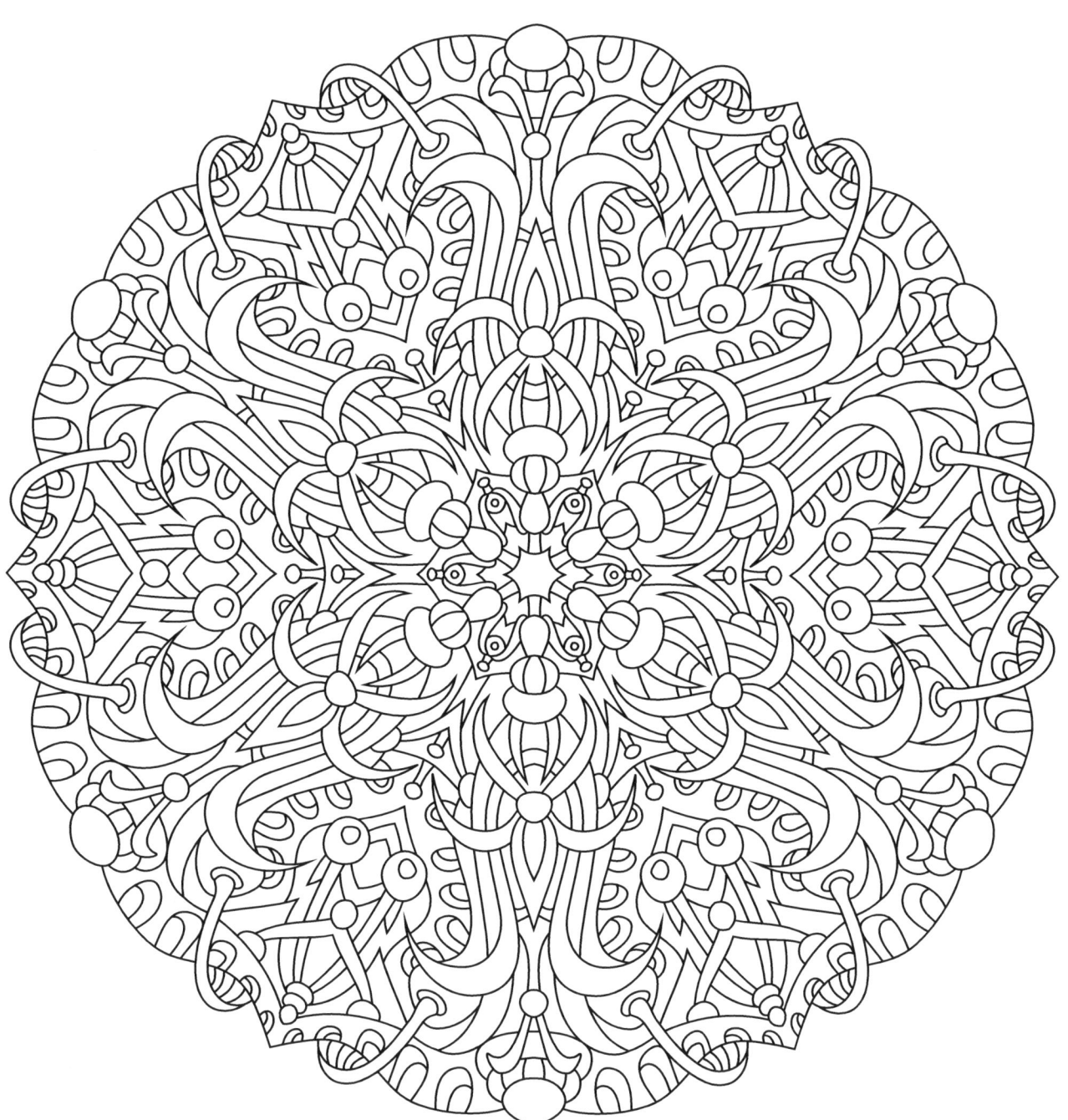

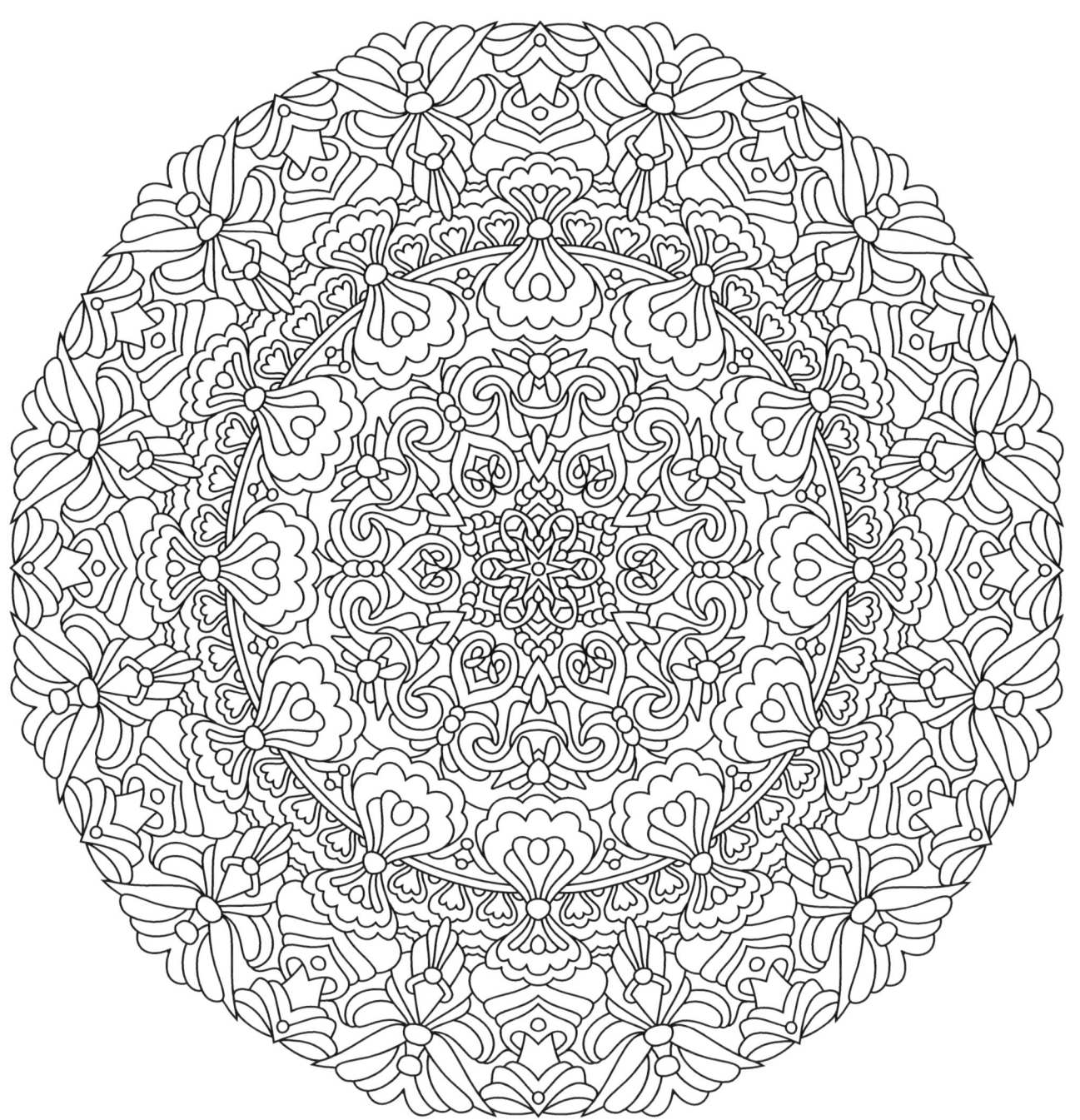

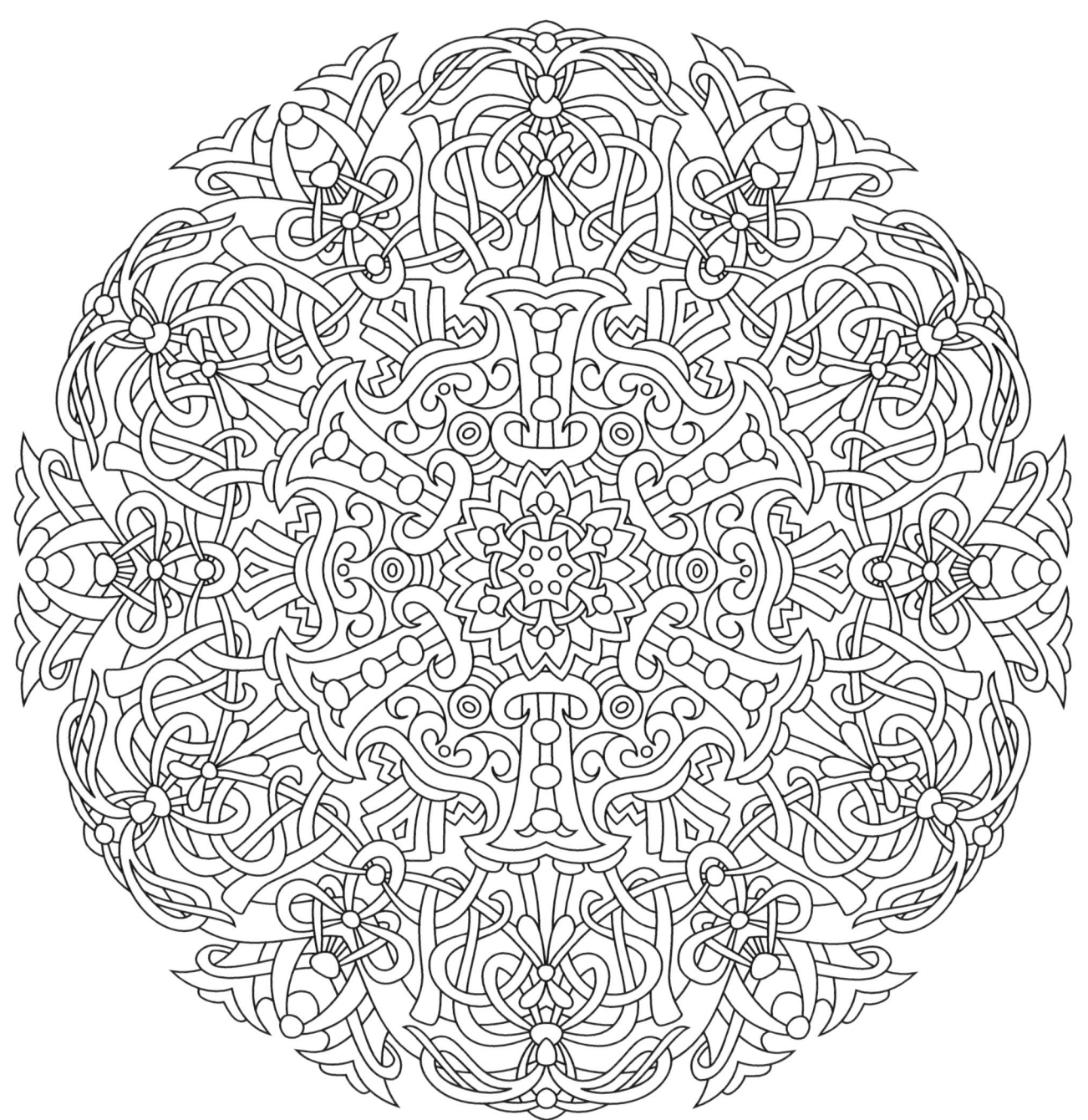

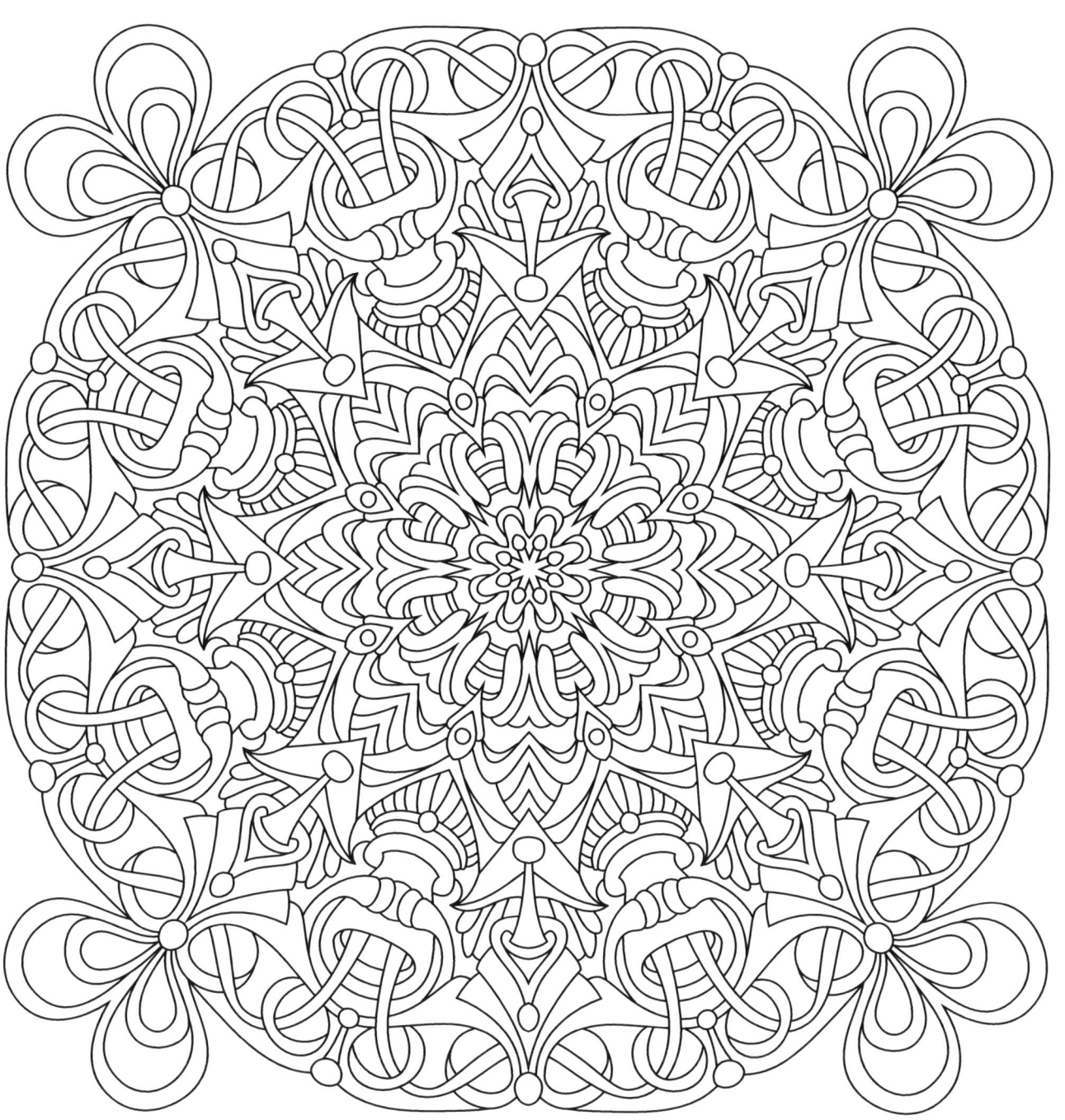

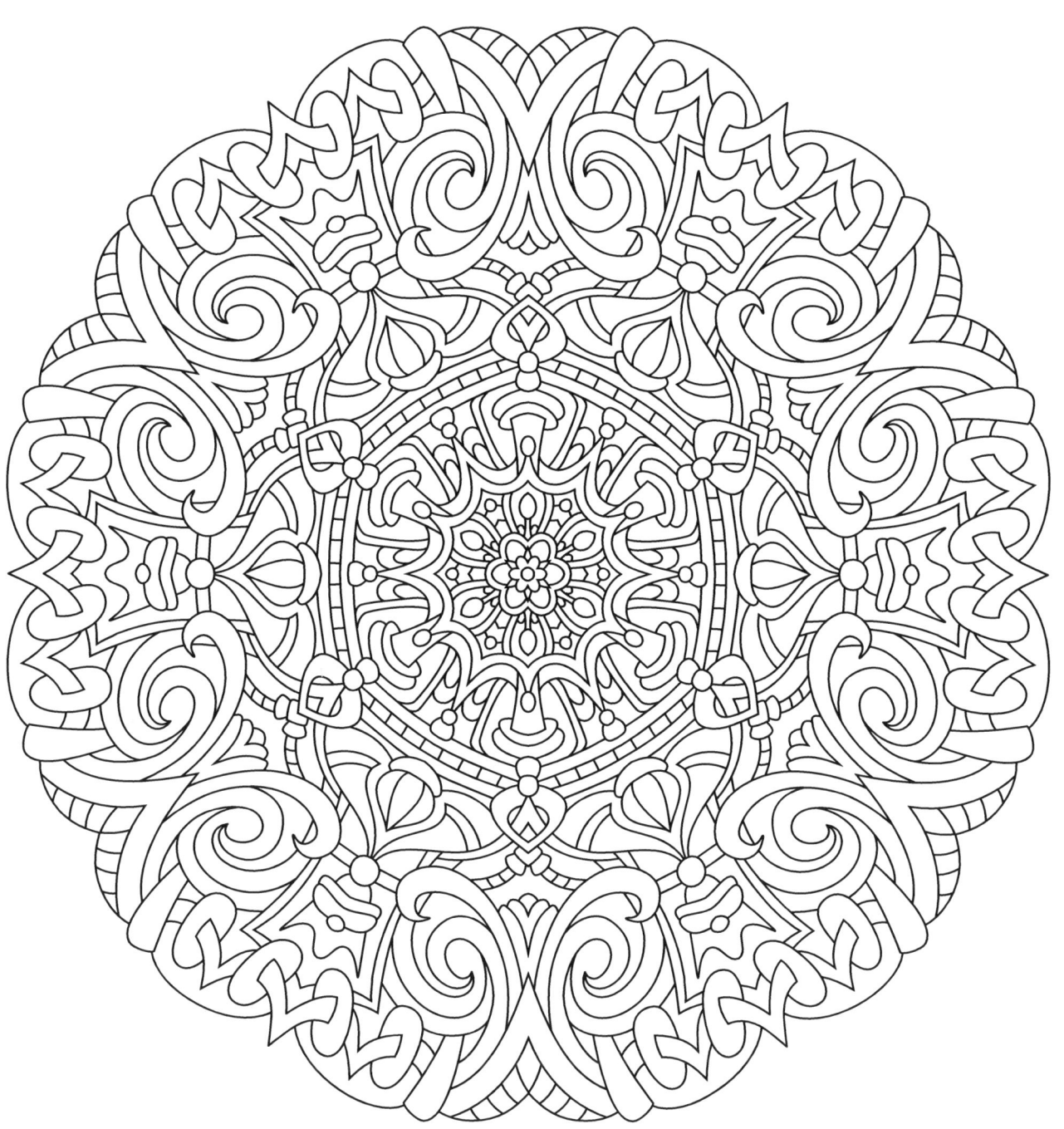

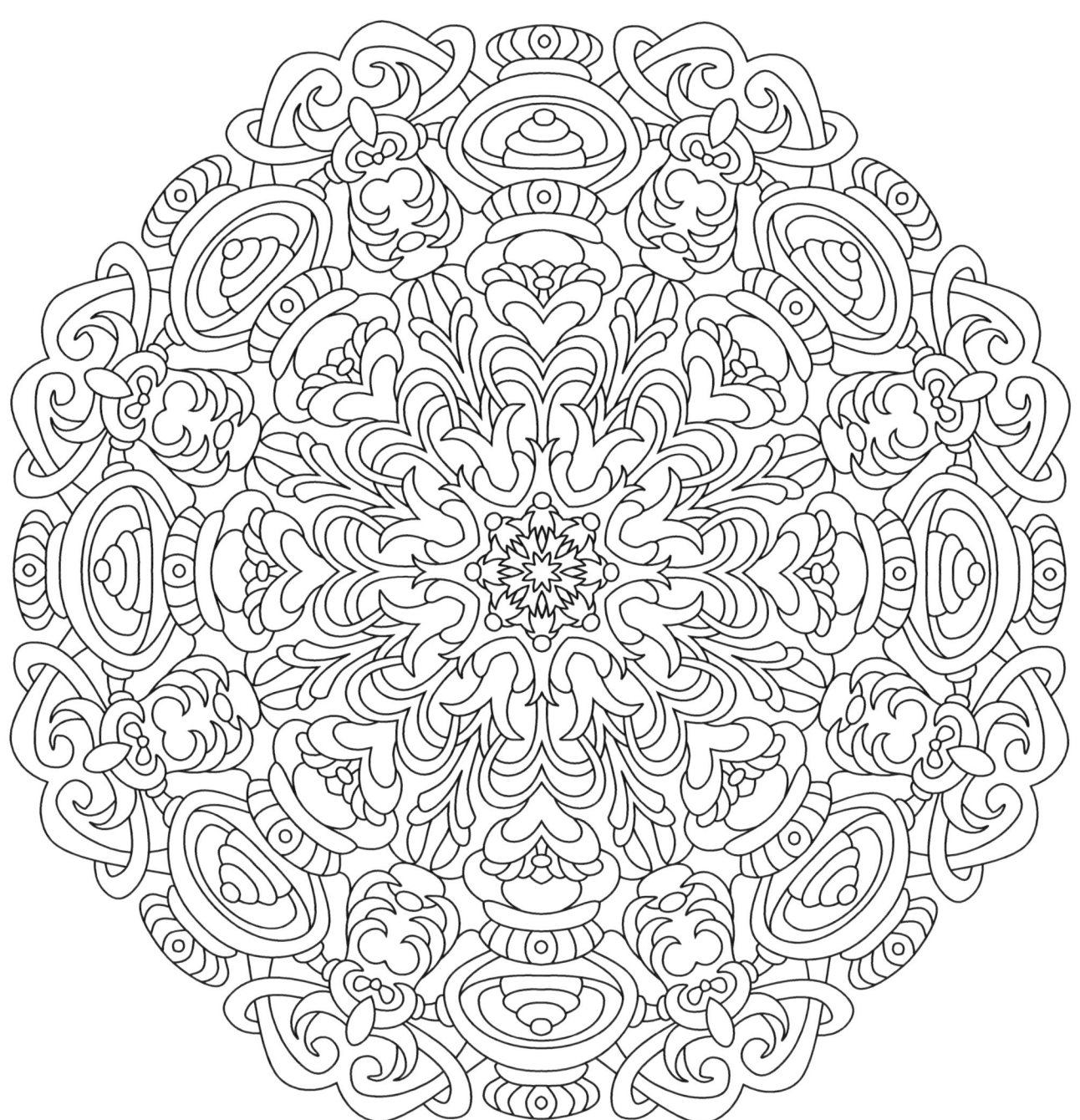

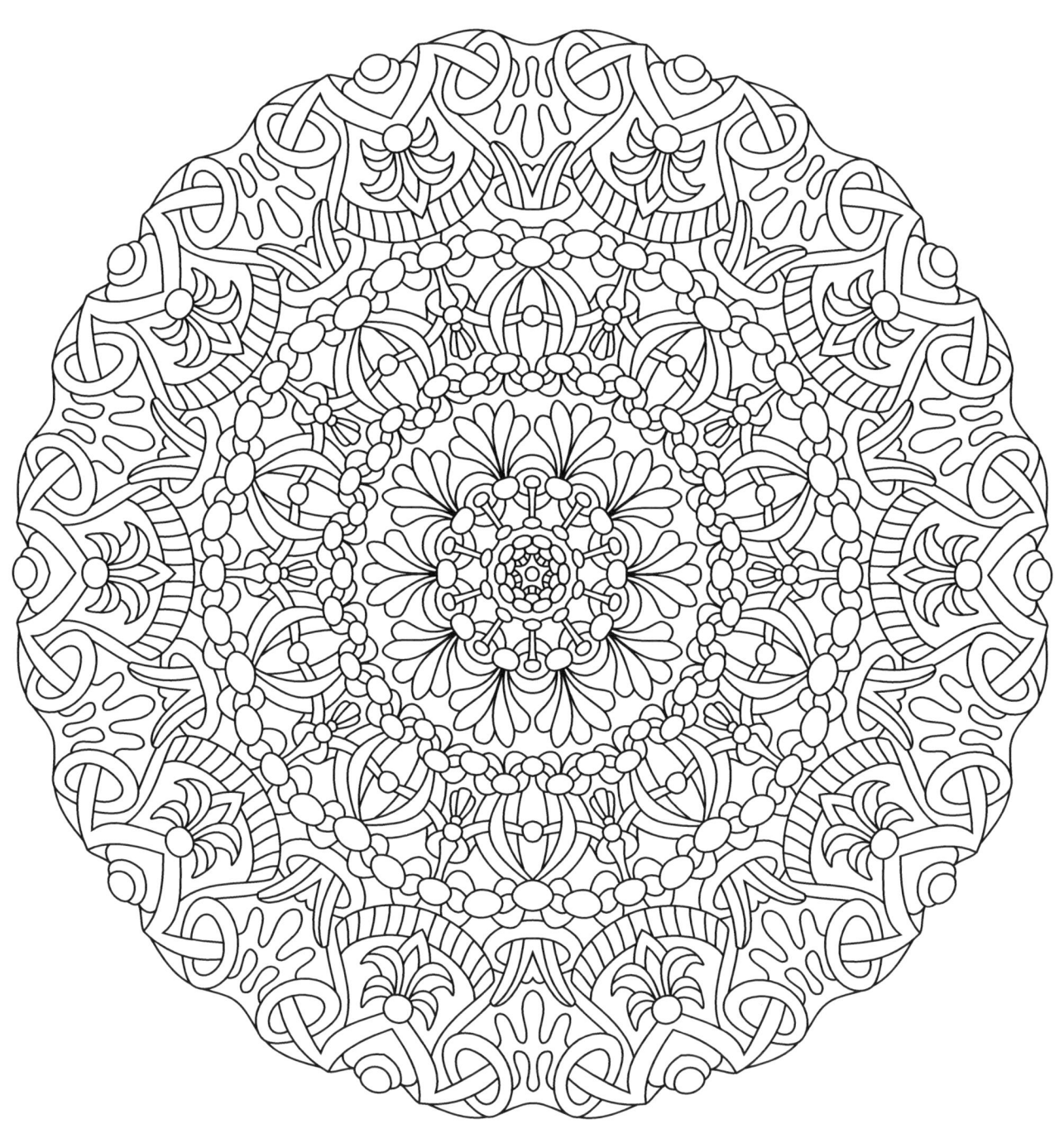

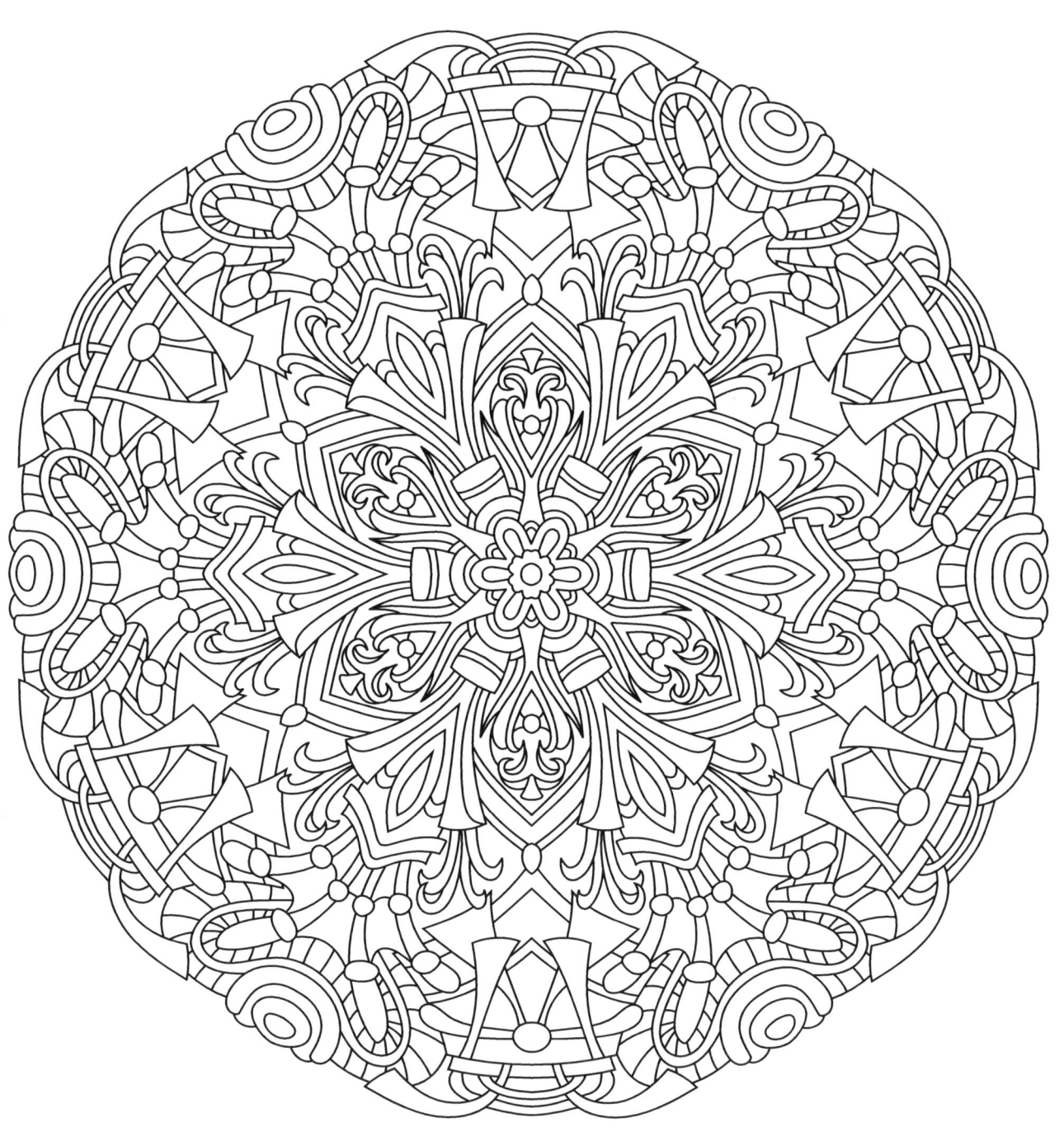

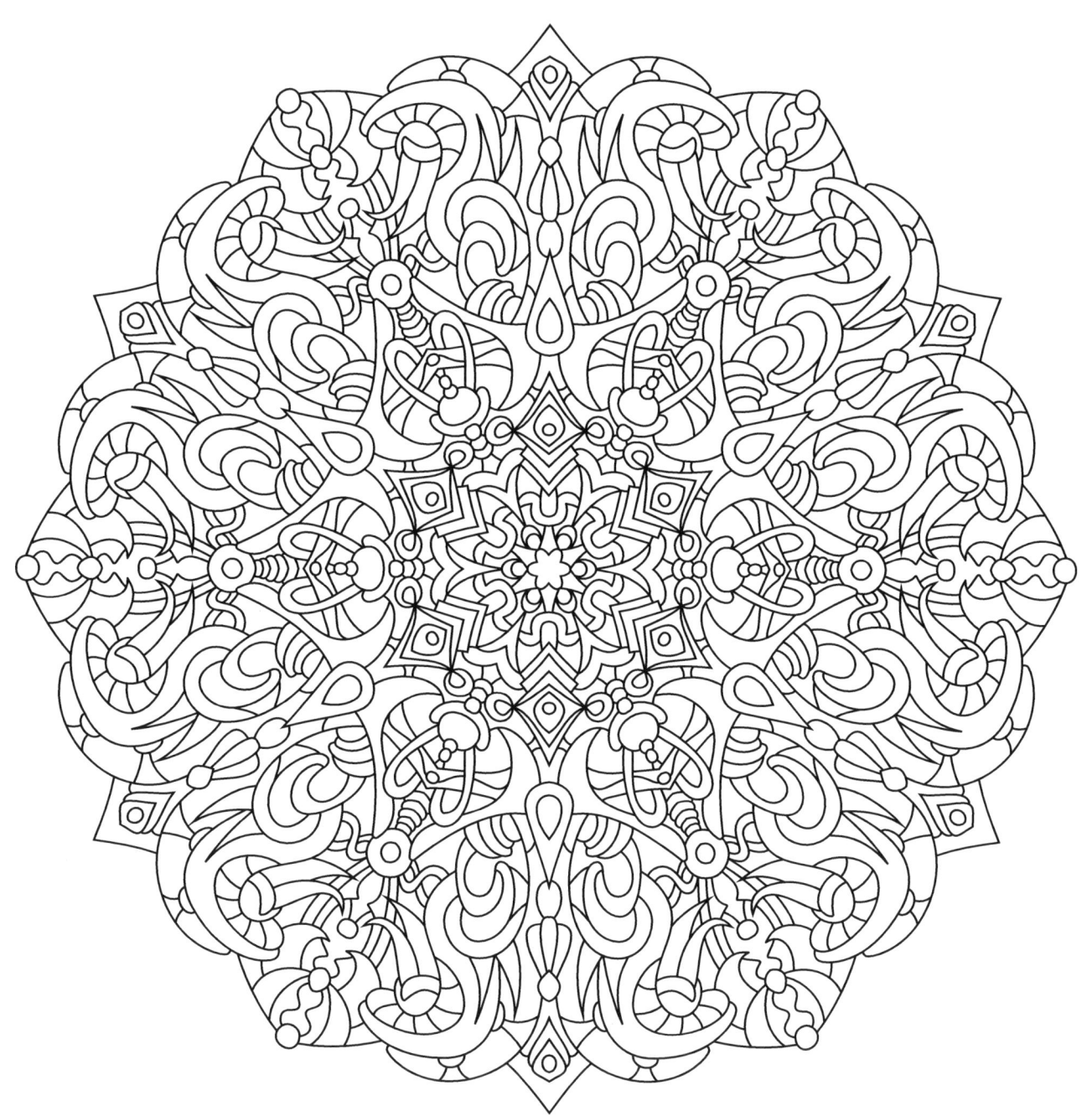

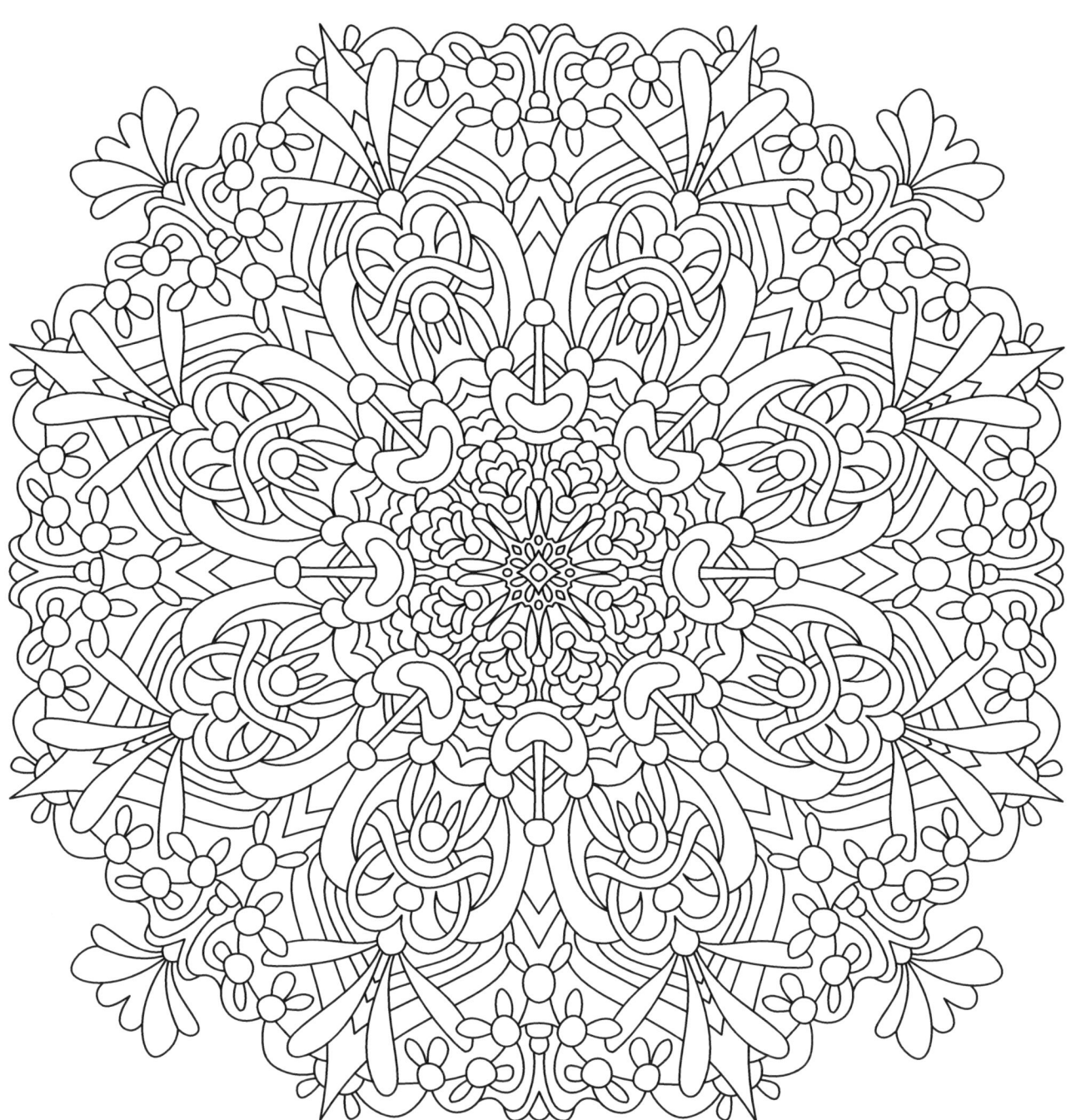

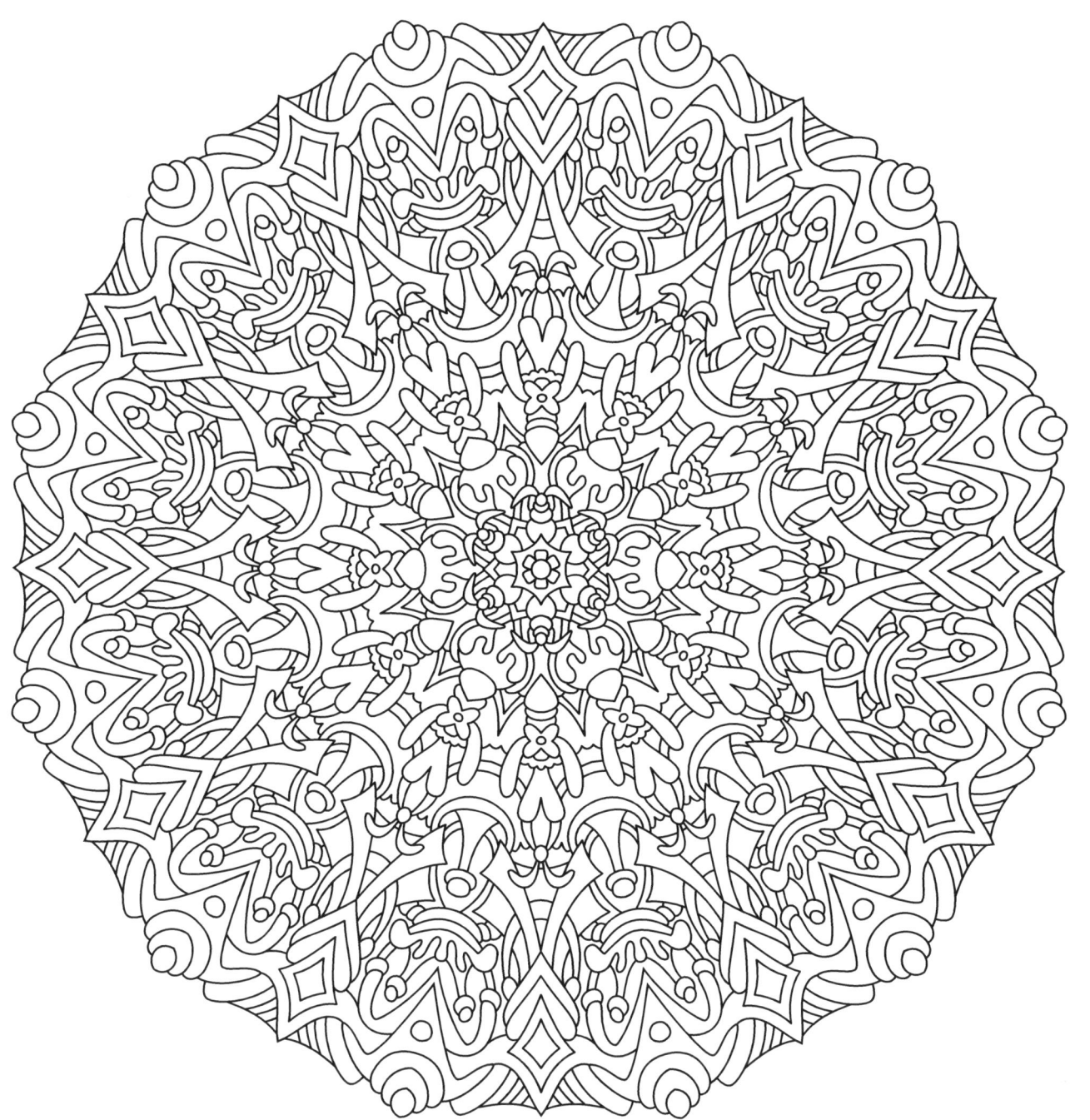

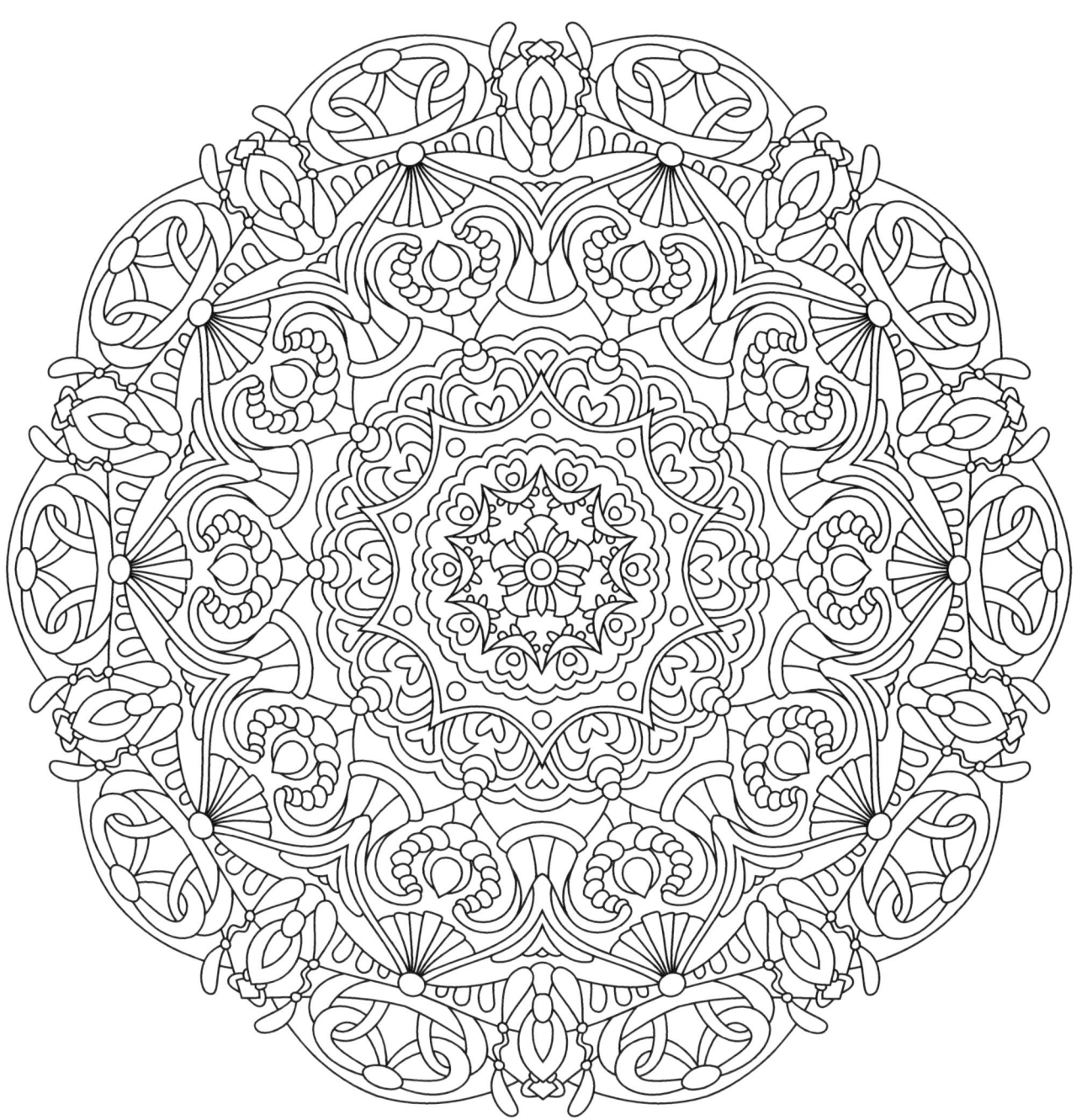

Visit Angie's website
for special web exclusives for colorists.

www.AngieGrace.com

62210531R00059

Made in the USA
Lexington, KY
01 April 2017